WORLD RELIGIONS

World
Religions

Michael Keene

Westminster John Knox Press
LOUISVILLE • LONDON

Text acknowledgments
The scripture quotations contained herein are from The New Revised Standard Version of the Bible, Anglicized Edition, copyright © 1989, 1995 by the Division of Christian Education of the National Council of the Churches of Christ in the United States of America, and are used by permission. All rights reserved.
Revised English Bible with the Apocrypha copyright © 1989 by Oxford University Press and Cambridge University Press.
Scriptures quoted from the Good News Bible are published by The Bible Societies/HarperCollins Publishers Ltd, UK © American Bible Society 1966, 1971, 1976, 1992, and used with permission.
Scripture quotations taken from the Holy Bible, New International Version, copyright

© 1973, 1978, 1984 by International Bible Society. Used by permission of Hodder & Stoughton Limited. All rights reserved. 'NIV' is a registered trademark of International Bible Society.

Picture acknowledgments
Please see page 192.

Contents

Note
Throughout this book the convention is followed of dating events by the abbreviations BCE (Before Common Era) and CE (Common Era). They correspond precisely to the more familiar BC and AD but avoid giving offence to those followers of non-Christian religions who do not recognize the birth of Christ as a decisive event in history.

Introducing World Religions

Even in our increasingly secular age religion plays a central role in the lives of millions of people. Studies suggest that over 70 per cent of the world's population identify themselves with one religion or another. Throughout Eastern Europe, for example, more and more people are going to worship at synagogues, mosques, temples and churches. In many parts of the world imams, rabbis and priests are working together to create a better, more peaceful world. At the same time, though, religious differences are often at the heart of much international and civil unrest – to which the former Yugoslavia, the Middle East and Northern Ireland bear eloquent testimony.

Religion shares in the most significant times and experiences of life. It celebrates birth, marks out the transition to adulthood, sets a seal on marriage and family life and eases the passage from one life to the next. For millions of people,

religion is there at the most special, and also the most frightening, moments of life. It also offers answers to those questions which perplex us. Is there a supreme power to whom we are answerable? How did life begin? What is it all about? Why do people suffer? What happens to us when we die? In the light of this it is probably not surprising that religion has provided the inspiration for much of the world's greatest art, music and literature.

This guide describes the main features of the world's six major religions, plus five other key faiths. It

presents all the information you need in a clear and user-friendly way, and the Rapid Factfinder allows easy access to words and concepts that are basic to each faith.

Hinduism stretches back thousands of years and is the oldest world religion still active today. There are millions of Hindu gods and goddesses and all are reflections of Brahman, the one supreme spirit. The most popular gods are Shiva, the destroyer, and Vishnu, the preserver.

Hundreds of temples are dedicated to them alone. All Hindus have shrines in their own homes, where they perform daily acts of worship, and these, together with festivals, form the heart of their faith. Their core belief is in an endless cycle of birth, life on earth, death and rebirth,

Each year millions of people make the pilgrimage to the holy city of Benares (Varanasi) in India to bathe in the River Ganges.

with each person being reincarnated at a level determined by how they spent their previous existence.

> *Do not do to another what you would not like to be done to yourself; that is the gist of the law — all other laws are variable.*
>
> MAHABHARATA, VEDA 39

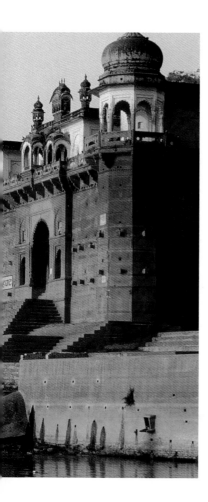

HINDUISM

Contents

Origins

Hinduism is rooted in the traditions and history of India and we can trace its origins back to the beginning of the second millennium BCE.

Hinduism originated in about 1800 BCE in India but its foundations are uncertain. Its earliest-known antecedents are in the Indus Valley civilization. The word itself comes from the Sanskrit for the River Indus, *Siddhu*, a word which the ancient Persians pronounced as 'Hindu'. It was not long before the word was applied generally to all the people of India, but today it just refers to the followers of the Hindu religion.

This statuette of Shiva, the destroyer, is full of symbolism. Together with Vishnu, the preserver, and Brahma, the creator-god, Shiva completes the Hindu trinity of gods, or *trimurti*. He is portrayed here as lord of the dance, celebrating the destruction of demons. The gesture made by one of his free hands indicates 'do not fear'.

The Indus people

We do not know much about the Indus Valley civilization. However, statues of goddesses from the time suggest that its people placed a heavy emphasis on the importance of female fertility. Some Hindu gods and goddesses, such as Shiva, are probably the descendants of these early deities.

After 300 years of relative peace, around 1500 BCE, Aryan tribes from the north-west overwhelmed the Indus people, and controlled India for the next millennium.

The Aryans

The Aryans brought the Sanskrit language with them. They also introduced the caste system, by which people were placed in different castes or varnas based on their occupation. Such social classification determined whom they were allowed to marry and socialize with. It did not take long for the caste system to become closely identified with Hinduism and it received support from some of its holy scriptures.

The Indus people and the Aryans intermarried and put together the *Vedas* – collections of hymns and writings. The earliest and most important of these books was the *Rig Veda*, in which praise was offered to

> *Hinduism is a living organism liable to growth and decay and subject to the laws of nature. One and indivisible at the root, it has grown into a vast tree with innumerable branches.*
>
> MAHATMA GANDHI (1869–1948), INDIAN POLITICAL LEADER

many gods including Indra, the god of heaven, Agni, the god of fire, and Aditi, the mother goddess. Forms of worship and spiritual discipline first mentioned in the *Vedas* are still an integral part of Hindu spirituality today.

Hinduism absorbed many ideas from other religions as it spread into southern India, much like a great river into which many tributaries flow. God was increasingly seen as a loving rather than an abstract deity, and this led to the writing of the much-loved Hindu spiritual classic, the *Bhagavad Gita*, which means *The Song of the Lord*.

The Caste System

The caste system has dominated social life in India for centuries and is supported by Hinduism's holy books. It is now illegal but caste distinctions still exert a great influence in the country areas of India.

According to Hindu tradition four varnas ('colours') were established by Brahman, the supreme god, at the time of creation. As time went on many tribes were influenced by Hinduism and a more complex caste system grew up. Castes are divisions in society based on people's occupations and thousands of castes and sub-castes remain in India.

Perusha

The four different varnas come from a story in the *Rig Veda* in which the god Brahma, who is in charge of creative power, makes the first man, Perusha. Perusha was later sacrificed and from his body the four varnas were taken:

◆ The highest (white) varna – the Brahmin – came from the mouth of Perusha. The Brahmins are priests who perform religious services and rituals and chant the scriptures.
◆ The second (red) varna – the Kshatriya – came from the arms of Perusha. This varna has produced the warriors and rulers of India.
◆ The third (yellow) varna – the Vaisya – came from Perusha's legs and produced those central to the economic and social life of the country, such as farmers and businesspeople.

Outcastes in India call themselves the Dalit – 'the oppressed'. About 20 per cent of Hindus – 110 million people – belong to this 'oppressed' caste.

THE 'UNTOUCHABLES'

The 'untouchables' do not belong to any caste and carry out the most menial tasks, such as tanning leather and burying the bodies of humans and animals. Mahatma Gandhi, the Hindu reformer, tried to raise the status of this large group by calling them Harijans, the 'children of God'. For centuries the 'untouchables' were banned from social life but this was outlawed in 1950. Hindu temples are now open to everyone, regardless of caste, and employment and educational opportunities are available to all. In India's village areas, though, the caste system still operates and marriage is almost always restricted to members of the same caste.

◆ The fourth (black) varna – the Sudra – came from Perusha's feet, which serve the rest of the body. This gave rise to the workers, who provide the basic services for others.

When they divided Primal Man how many divisions did they make? What was his mouth? What his arms? The Brahmin was his mouth. The Kshatriya his arms. His thighs the Vaisya. The Sudra from his feet.

RIG VEDA, BOOK 10

A Brahmin in a shrine at Calcutta. The Brahmin acts as an intermediary between the worshipper and the god.

Belief in God

Hinduism is a monotheistic religion whose adherents believe in one God, Brahman (the absolute spirit), who is beyond human reach and understanding. There are millions of different images that make Brahman visible and knowable to worshippers.

Not all of Hinduism's millions of followers believe in God. These 'secular Hindus' recognize the importance of the principle of order in the universe — that summer follows spring, night follows day and harvest follows seedtime. They look to Hinduism to guarantee this but they do not hold to the religion's mythology.

Brahman

The vast majority of Hindus, however, do believe in God — or should we say 'gods'? Hindu teaching is far from clear on this point and even the holy books give conflicting messages. The *Rig Veda*, for example, refers to 33 gods, although elsewhere the same book denies that they have real existence. The truth seems to be that there is one God in Hinduism who can be worshipped under many different forms and guises. The one God is Brahman.

Brahman is the ultimate reality, supreme spirit, beyond

all human understanding, time and space. While Brahman is found throughout the universe he is beyond it. He is the origin of all creation – pure intelligence, pure delight and pure being. Brahman is the entire world around us – and yet he is our inner world as well.

> *God is the primary cause of all true knowledge and of everything known by its means. God is All-truth, All-knowledge, All-beatitude, Incorporeal, Almighty, Just, Merciful, Unbegotten, Infinite, Unchangeable, Without a beginning, Incomparable, the Support and Lord of all, All-pervading, Omniscient, Imperishable, Immortal, Exempt from fear, Eternal, Holy and the Cause of the universe. To him alone is worship due.*
>
> TEN PRINCIPLES OF THE ARYA SAMAJ

There is one God in Hinduism, Brahman, who takes many visible forms.

This inner world is called the atman, the soul, and Brahman and the atman are one, although human beings do not always realize this. Heaven is reached and the cycle of birth, life and death ended when Brahman and the soul are reunited.

Gods and goddesses

Hinduism's many gods and goddesses make it a wonderfully colourful religion. They also illuminate different aspects of Brahman's character. The *Rig Veda* explains, 'To what is one, sages give many a name, Agni, Yama, Matarisvan…' and another holy book adds, 'For an awakened soul, Indra, Agni, Aditya, Candra, all these names represent one basic power and spiritual reality.'

In Hinduism God is neither male nor female, but, since Brahman embraces all of creation, he can take male, female or animal form. Many gods are given consorts to demonstrate this. Brahma, the creator-god, for example, is always mentioned alongside Saraswati, the goddess of learning. In fact, Saraswati has become much more popular with worshippers than Brahma!

Images of God

The many qualities present in Brahman are revealed to the world in the images of millions of gods and goddesses. These images allow worshippers to know the 'unknowable'.

Hindus believe that the supreme being, Brahman, controls the world through the three major qualities which are represented in the *trimurti* – Brahma, Vishnu and Shiva – a triad which developed in Hinduism about 2,000 years ago. Brahma is rarely worshipped today but Vishnu has millions of followers. Hindus believe that Vishnu visits the earth as an avatar – 'one who descends' or 'incarnation' – whenever evil reaches an unacceptable level. Nine out of the 10 promised avatars of Vishnu have already taken place.

Each Hindu temple and home has a shrine to its own special god. Hanuman, the monkey-god, represents dexterity and intelligence.

Krishna

Vishnu's most popular avatar took the form of a cow-herd, Krishna, whom many Hindus worship as a god in his own right. There are many stories in the holy books illustrating Krishna's fame as a lover, soldier and ruler. Krishna's occupation partly explains why the cow is a sacred animal to Hindus and therefore never slaughtered.

Rama

Rama is another well-known avatar of Vishnu. The Lord Rama is the hero of the *Ramayana*, one of Hinduism's greatest epic poems. Rama defeated the demon-king Ravana, the ruler of Sri Lanka, who had abducted his wife, Sita, and he called on Hanuman, the popular monkey-god, to help him. Many Hindus today revere Hanuman as a symbol of strength and energy.

Ganesha

Ganesha, the elephant-god, is one of the best-loved Hindu deities. Ganesha was the first-born son of Shiva and his beautiful wife, Parvati. On returning home after a long absence Shiva saw a stranger in

It is estimated that there are as many as 330 million deities in Hinduism. The vast majority of them, however, are redundant and no longer have any worshippers.

> *In my early youth I was taught to repeat what in Hindu scriptures are known as the 1,000 names of God. But these 1,000 names of God were by no means exhaustive. We believe — and I think it is the truth — that God has as many names as there are creatures and, therefore, we also say that God is nameless and, since God has many forms, we also consider him formless and, since he speaks through many tongues, we consider him speechless.*
>
> MAHATMA GANDHI (1869–1948),
> INDIAN POLITICAL LEADER

Animal characteristics point to the special qualities of the gods. Ganesha, the elephant-god, symbolizes strength and protection.

his house and cut off his head. Discovering that he had killed his own son, Shiva then cut the head off an elephant and placed it on his son's shoulders. For Hindus, Ganesha's large elephant head and ears represent the gaining of knowledge through reflection and listening, while the two tusks, one perfectly shaped and the other broken, represent perfection and imperfection, which are present everywhere in the world. Ganesha symbolizes strong leadership; he's the one who removes obstacles and he's the repository of wisdom and perfection. It is perhaps not surprising that Hindus offer Ganesha worship before embarking on a new business venture or setting up a new home.

Beliefs

Over its long history Hinduism has attracted and absorbed many ideas from other religions. Hindus do not all believe the same thing, although there are central tenets which most people accept.

The Hindu understanding of human life centres on the relationship between the body and the soul, or atman. The body belongs to the material world, which is always changing and is imperfect, whereas the atman is part of the spiritual reality of Brahman – perfect, unchanging and the ultimate truth.

Samsara

'Samsara' means 'wandering' and refers to the wandering of the soul from body to body,

COW VENERATION

Gandhi, the Indian reformer, once remarked that the cow is really the most universal Hindu symbol and cow protection its most expressive principle. Hindus may agree on little else but they do look upon the veneration of the cow as a token of nonviolence. All of a cow's products – including milk, urine and dung – are seen as purifying.

lifetime after lifetime, from birth, through life, to death. It is comparable to new buds appearing on a tree each spring, even though the tree appears to have died the previous winter. For Hindus both the natural world and human nature are subject to the same 'recycling'.

Karma

The reason why all living things are continually being reborn is karma, the law of cause and effect. Hindus believe that the karma accumulated in previous lives is carried over into the present and so determines the state of the soul's rebirth. Each Hindu seeks to remove the effect of karma on their next rebirth by living a life of charity and selfless action. The *Bhagavad Gita* teaches that this is the only way to be reborn with less karma. Evil karma will ensure that a person's atman returns at a lower level in the next life.

Moksha

Moksha is the end of samsara and is the goal of every Hindu. Hindu spirituality is mainly concerned with carrying the human soul to 'the other shore', in other words, teaching ways to find liberation from rebirth. To do this Hindus need to neutralize karma by detaching themselves from all desire. It is like extracting gold from its metal impurities: it takes many attempts but eventually pure gold is obtained. At the end of this process the atman is reabsorped into the divine – Brahman.

Hindus frequently use the image of a river at the end of its journey flowing into, and being swallowed up by, the sea. This can only happen to the atman when it becomes totally pure and unaffected by anything that happens in life on earth. Then the soul can return to being part of Brahman – which is where it began.

As a man casts off his worn-out clothes, and takes other new ones in their place, so does the embodied soul cast off his worn-out bodies, and enter others anew.
BHAGAVAD GITA

Hindus believe it may take as many as 8,400,000 rebirths before the atman is able to escape the trap of samsara.

A holy man, or sadhu, in front of a banner of Shiva.

19

Holy Books

Hinduism's sacred books were written over many time periods and employ various writing forms. They range from obscure philosophical texts to epic legends and stories.

The sacred writings of Hinduism are divided into two broad groups: the *Shrutis* and the *Smritis*.

Shruti

The *Shrutis* ('that which is heard') are seen as divine in origin. They contain the ancient hymns of the *Vedas*, which were written late in the second millennium BCE in Sanskrit, the ancient language of India. The *Rig Veda*, the earliest and most sacred, is a book of 1,028 poems reflecting the nomadic life of the Aryans as they charged into battle, rejoiced in the sun rising each morning and reflected on the loneliness of a silent evening.

The *Upanishads* come at the end of the *Vedas*. The books' title refers to the disciple who sits at the feet of the Guru to gain wisdom. The *Upanishads* record 120 conversations between teacher and disciple and contain the most important Hindu teaching of all – that of Brahman and the atman.

> *Let your mother be a god to you.*
> *Let your father be a god to you.*
> *Let your teacher be a god to you.*
> *Let your guest be a god to you.*
> *Let only those works be done by you that are free from blemishes.*
> *Only deeds that are good are to be performed by you.*
> TAITTIRIYA UPANISHAD I:XI:1–2

Smriti

The *Smritis* ('that which is remembered') are holy books of human origin. They contain the tales told by trained storytellers. The *Ramayana*, a 48,000-line poem, tells the story of Rama and Sita and is a source of great spiritual instruction and advice to Hindus.

With 100,000 verses the *Mahabharata* is the longest poem in any language and there is a saying that what is not in this epic is not in India. It describes the war between two families, the Pandavas and the Kauravas, who were cousins. The Pandavas were five

The *Vedas* were written down between 1500 and 800 BCE. They are the oldest-known books.

This illustration from the *Bhagavad Gita* depicts the enlightening conversation between the Lord Krishna (right) and Arjuna on the battlefield.

brothers renowned for their faith in God while the Kauravas were a family of 100 evil-minded brothers.

THE *BHAGAVAD GITA*

The *Bhagavad Gita* is part of the *Mahabharata* and is the best-loved spiritual classic in Hinduism. It takes the form of a conversation on the battlefield between the Lord Krishna and the hero Arjuna, during which Arjuna learns about the immortality of the soul, the duty of the warrior caste to fight and the need to do your duty to the best of your ability.

A historic battle was fought between them in the Punjab which the Pandavas won, representing the ultimate victory of good over evil. The *Mahabharata* teaches that righteousness is the source of progress in a nation while wickedness leads to its eventual destruction.

The Temple

For many Hindus the temple is the centre of religious life. For others, however, communal acts of worship are not important and they rarely visit a temple.

Each Hindu temple, or *mandir*, is dedicated to a particular god, often Krishna, and a statue of the god is kept in a special room, the *garbhagrha*. People worship together in the main part of the temple, the *mandapa*. The priest enters the *garbhagrha* to wash and dress the image of the god and present it with flowers, incense, fruit and other gifts. After this the curtains which separate the *mandapa* and *garbhagrha* are drawn back so that worshippers can present their own gifts to the god. The *garbhagrha* usually has a roof which is shaped like a tower and represents a mountain – considered a sacred part of nature by Hindus. The ceiling is often beautifully carved or decorated with tinsel and small lights. Although the temple is dedicated to one god it symbolizes the whole of the cosmos.

Worship in the temple

While most Hindu worship takes place at home many Hindus visit their local temple regularly. Here worshippers offer their devotion, or *bhakti*, by lighting a candle and saying prayers and, as they leave, each of them is given *prashad* (sacred food) which has been offered to the god earlier in the day. In the evening a retire-to-bed ceremony is carried out by the priest to the accompaniment of bells and drums during which the statue is again washed and then put to rest for the night.

Group worship (*puja*) also happens in the temple and this takes one of three forms:

Temples are frequently covered with representations of the gods and are rich in symbolism.

◆ The singing of a hymn, or *Bhajan*, involves the playing of bells and tambourines while some people dance. Dancing is an important aspect of Hindu worship and is deeply symbolic. The priest reads from the *Bhagavad Gita* before ending the service with the prayer for peace: 'O God let there be peace, peace, peace.'

◆ *Arti* is the welcoming service. For this the priest places five candles on a tray to represent the five elements of fire, earth, air, ether and water. Worshippers pass their hands over the flames and then over their heads to receive God's power and blessing.

◆ *Havan* is the offering of fire. Using wood, camphor and ghee

*Whatever a zealous soul may offer,
be it a leaf, fruit or water,
that I willingly accept
for it was given in love.*
BHAGAVAD GITA

the priest kindles a fire on a portable fire-altar, to represent the mouth of the god devouring the offerings in front of him. Sections of the *Vedas* are recited and the priest and people ceremonially wash themselves to symbolize their purity in God's sight.

Temple worship involves chanting mantras to summon the gods, prayers, singing and listening to teaching. The offering of gifts has an important place in worship.

Worshipping God

Hinduism helps its followers to worship God in three unique ways – through the sacred syllable, the singing of mantras and the use of mandalas.

Many Hindus worship at home only, while some worship both at home and in the temple and others worship in the temple only.

The sacred syllable

The sacred syllable, *AUM* or *OM*, first crops up in the sacred collection of books, the *Upanishads*, and is made up of three sounds – 'a', 'u' and 'm' – together with a humming undercurrent. Hindus believe that, when spoken, this threefold sound represents:

The sacred *AUM* syllable. Traditionally, *AUM* was the first sound, out of which the universe arose.

◆ the first three *Vedas*.
◆ the three worlds – earth, atmosphere and heaven.
◆ the three main gods – Brahma, Vishnu and Shiva.

For many Hindus, however, the sacred syllable represents more than this. They understand its sound to embrace the whole universe and its oneness with God. It is understood as a great affirmative statement about God,

along the lines of: 'Yes, there is an eternal being behind the ever-changing world.'

Hindus like to have the sacred syllable visible in their homes and it is often found on such everyday objects as paperweights. It concludes religious works, acts of worship and any important task, as well as being placed at the beginning and end of all Hindu books.

Mantras

Mantras play a vital role in all Hindu worship – as they do for many Buddhists. A mantra is a verse, syllable or series of syllables which is believed to have divine origin.

> *Meditation on this sacred syllable satisfies every need and finally leads to liberation.*
> KATHA UPANISHAD, 2:16, 17
>
> *OM. The imperishable sound is the seed of all that exists. The past, the present, the future, are all but the unfolding of the OM.*
> MANDUKYA UPANISHAD

THE MANDALA

A mandala is a complex geometric pattern, used in worship, to involve the entire cosmos. For important rituals a mandala is traced on consecrated ground using coloured powders, then obliterated afterwards. The spaces in the mandala represent the most popular gods or personal deities, with Vishnu in the middle.

It is repeated over and over again to raise the worshipper's consciousness and awareness of God. It is believed the mantra can bring release from the mundane and trivial matters that normally occupy the mind into an altogether different spiritual realm. Hindus often chant a mantra quietly on their way to work.

A priest performing an act of worship, or *puja*. Most Hindu worship takes place at home, and even the poorest families have a place for *puja* of their favourite gods.

Worship at Home

The family is the basic unit in Hindu society and is responsible for safeguarding Hindu traditions and customs. A very important part of this duty is the proper and appropriate worship of the family deity.

Most Hindu worship takes place in the home rather than at the *mandir*. Each home has a shrine containing a picture of the family god — often Krishna, who is known for the love and kindness he showed on his visit to earth as an avatar of Vishnu.

Hindu children are brought up to observe the five daily duties:

◆ to perform some yoga or meditation.

A Hindu woman standing in front of her home shrine. Offerings of incense, flowers, food and drink are made each day to the household's favourite deities.

◆ to show reverence and offer worship to the family god.

◆ to show an unquestioning respect for family elders and ancestors.

◆ to extend the hospitality of the family to all those who are needy as well as to holy men and women.

◆ to show respect for all living creatures.

Acts of worship

Women carry the heaviest spiritual responsibility in a Hindu home. It is up to them to ensure all necessary religious rituals are carried out and that festivals are celebrated appropriately. Hinduism has a strong storytelling tradition and women make sure the best stories are handed down from generation to generation.

Each morning the woman of the house rises early, takes a bath while chanting God's name and puts on clean clothes. She worships God by washing, dressing or decorating the image of the family god before offering it flowers, fruit and incense. Other members of the family then follow her example. She lights a lamp which has had its wick dipped in ghee. Incense sticks are lit and the names of God are repeated along with the daily prayer – the *Gyatri Mantra* – which declares, 'Let us meditate on the glorious light of the creator. May he guide our minds and inspire us with understanding.'

A reading from one of the holy books often takes place in front of a mandala, during which time the worshippers sit upright and cross-legged on the floor, breathing deeply to aid concentration. The sacred Hindu syllable, *AUM* or *OM*, is chanted over and over again as people pass their hands over the flame of the lamp to share in the power and energy of God.

> *The worship of an image is the art of embracing the whole universe in a little object.*
> VINOBA BHAVE
> (1895–1982),
> INDIAN RELIGIOUS
> FIGURE

Ceremonies

There are 16 ceremonies, or samskaras, marking the most important stages of life – from pre-conception to death. If the correct rituals are carried out then the bad effects of karma can be cancelled and a better rebirth obtained in the next life.

The first three samskaras are carried out before birth. Number one is performed before conception, when a couple prays that they might be able to have a child. The second, at the start of pregnancy, asks that both mother and baby will be kept safe from evil spirits. After seven months of pregnancy, the third is believed to ensure the continued health of mother and child. Immediately after birth the baby is washed, the sacred syllable is traced on the tongue, with a golden pen dipped in honey, and a symbolic mark is made on the infant's forehead.

Name-giving
The baby's name is kept secret until the 11th or 12th day after birth, in case evil spirits try to carry him or her away before the protection of the next samskara is given. The priest ties scarlet threads to the baby to symbolize this protection and places a piece of gold in the baby's hands as a sign of good fortune ahead.

> *Worn-out garments are shed by the body, worn-out bodies are shed by the dweller, within the body new bodies are donned by the dweller, like garments.*
> *BHAGAVAD GITA, 2:22*

The child's horoscope is drawn up and he or she is named using two or three letters from their zodiac sign at the beginning. For boys another samskara follows shortly afterwards: their hair is cut off and weighed and its equivalent in gold is given to the poor.

The sacred thread
The sacred thread, or *upanayana*, is the 10th and most significant samskara, in which the priest places a thread across a boy's shoulder. It takes place between the ages of five and eight for the sons of Brahmins and later for members of lower castes. The ceremony marks the time when the boy passes into the hands of a Guru for his religious instruction.

Marriage
Marriage marks the beginning of the status of 'householder' and is the 13th samskara. The wedding ceremony is carried out around a sacred fire and is full of symbolism. During the service the couple take seven steps around the fire with their hands clasped, making a promise to each other with each step. *The Laws of Manu*, a holy book, say that a wife must always love and respect her husband, and orthodox Hindus do not accept divorce under any circumstances.

Death
Anyesti, the final samskara, is the funeral ceremony. By tradition the eldest son leads the funeral party to the place of cremation and the youngest son leads the party back home. Each Hindu hopes to die within reach of the River Ganges so that their bones and ashes can be lowered into the water – so ending the cycle of rebirth.

A body is cremated on one of the steps, or ghats, lining the banks of the Ganges. If a family is unable to cremate its dead by a holy river, it will instead scatter the ashes on water, along with sacred marigold flowers.

Festivals

Hinduism is a religion of many festivals, although the vast majority are only celebrated locally. Festivals are seen to guarantee the continuation of Hindu traditions and help children to learn about the gods.

Hindu religious festivals can be divided into three groups.

Festivals based on the Hindu calendar

The first group is based on the Hindu calendar, which follows a pattern of six seasons over a year of 354 days. Each lasts for two months, and they are: spring (March to May); summer (May to July); the rainy season (July to September); autumn (September to November); winter (November to January) and the good season (January to March). Divali, the Festival of Lights, takes place over five days in October or November and is the most widely celebrated Hindu festival. For many Divali is the time to welcome Lakshmi, the goddess of prosperity and happiness, into their home.

Dassehra is also held in October or November and celebrates the goodness of the gods. Any arguments or disagreements are dealt with before the festival ends, creating a sense of well-being in the community.

Saraswati is named after the popular goddess of learning and knowledge and can be celebrated at any time. A statue of the goddess as a beautiful

In 2001 the Kumbh Mela brought together over 20 million pilgrims who gathered at Prayag. On the great day of the Mela 10 million of them bathed at the point where the River Ganges meets the River Jamuna.

HOLI

The festival of *Holi* is held in the spring and centres on the activities of Krishna on his visit to earth as an avatar. By now the spring harvest is safely gathered in, so *Holi* is a time of much enjoyment. An important festival activity is the throwing of coloured dye over other people. This is followed by an act of *puja* before the midday meal when a portion of food is thrown into the flames of a small bonfire as an act of thanksgiving.

Hindu women throwing dye over each other during the festival of *Holi*. *Holi* is a time of fun and playfulness, and caste distinctions are temporarily put aside as members of lower castes are permitted to throw dye or paint over those of higher castes.

woman riding a swan is carried through the streets.

Festivals linked to agricultural seasons

The second group comprises festivals linked to specific seasons in the agricultural year. In a country so dependent on agriculture, the times of sowing and reaping are the most vital in the year. *Navaratri*, the 'nine-nights festival', celebrates the sowing of the winter crops. At the start of the festival some barley is sown on a small dish so that by the end it has started to sprout.

Melas

The third group of festivals celebrates important events in Hindu legend known as *melas*. The Kumbh Mela is held every 12 years and circulates around four different centres: Haridwar, Nasik, Prayaga and Ujjain. The myth behind the celebration is of a battle between the gods and the demons over a jug which held the nectar of immortality. The gods were victorious, but during the battle four drops of nectar were spilled on the sites where the Kumbh Mela is held.

Paths to Salvation

There are four recognized religious paths or ways of finding personal salvation. It is up to each person to choose the path they take, although some are much more difficult than others.

The four paths to personal salvation in Hinduism are the means by which an individual might find eventual release from the seemingly endless cycle of birth, life and death.

The path of *bhakti*
Bhakti is loving devotion to one of the gods. The domestic shrine found in every Hindu home has a very important part to play in *bhakti* since it is here that each Hindu offers *puja* as an act of personal devotion. Hymn-singing, telling the stories of the gods, religious drama, dancing and celebrating the religious festivals are all key elements of the *bhakti* tradition.

The path of karma
According to the *Bhagavad Gita* the moral law of existence is that good deeds bear good fruit while bad deeds bear bad fruit – the law of karma. This acts like a chain of cause and effect since the way a person lives in one existence affects how they return in the next.

> *Whatever you do, eat, offer as an oblation, give as a gift or undertake as a penance, offer all that to Me.*
> LORD KRISHNA

Hindus believe that everything a person does affects their karma so every human being must take care to do only actions which produce good karma.

The path of *jnana*
Jnana is the most difficult path for a person to walk to salvation. It not only requires constant guidance from a spiritual Guru, but also the ability to understand all the holy scriptures – an almost impossible task. Only a few people have ever been able to free themselves from attachment to this world through a clear understanding of the scriptures.

The path of yoga
Yoga is a spiritual discipline of physical and mental exercises

There are eight separate stages in the Hindu approach to yoga. This includes 86 different positions for the body. In the last stage of contemplation, or samadhi, the person is likened to a lotus flower in a dirty pond, untouched by the surrounding grime. Beyond this lies only moksha – liberation.

A Hindu holy man following a path which he hopes will lead to liberation, or moksha. He wears minimal clothing, fasts and performs yoga as penance. He is supported by gifts of food and money from laypeople.

which have been practised in India for thousands of years. They are intended to give a person control over his or her own mind and body. The ancient holy books set out a number of requirements for people who wish to use yoga to break their attachment to this world. They must show self-control, nonviolence, truthfulness and chastity, and avoid greed. They must master certain yoga positions, the most important of which is the lotus position – the art of sitting cross-legged with feet resting on thighs. Breathing exercises also aid concentration, as does focusing the mind on a statue of a god. Mantras can also be sung to lead the mind forward and so raise its awareness of its own oneness with the supreme spirit, Brahman.

Pilgrimage

Although Hindus are not under any obligation to make a pilgrimage to the holy places of their faith, many choose to do so. Making such a journey, often over long distances and involving real hardship, helps a pilgrim to grow in inner, spiritual strength. It is also a way of showing devotion and love to God.

Hindus make pilgrimages as part of their spiritual journey for a variety of reasons: to carry out a spiritual vow they have made to a chosen deity; to make amends for breaking a religious law; to offer thanksgiving for the birth of a baby; to gain religious merit; to purify themselves; or simply to express devotion to a deity. Others undertake a pilgrimage to fulfil the wishes of a late family member; most Hindus want their ashes scattered on the waters of a sacred river in the hope that this might bring them nearer to escaping from the cycle of rebirth. A pilgrimage also provides an

Pilgrims washing in the River Ganges, an act believed to have religious merit and to bring salvation closer. Ritual ablutions are accompanied by prayers to the sun.

There are 24 major pilgrimage sites in India, of which the four located on the exact points of the compass are the most significant. These are the abodes of the gods. They are the Jagannath temple at Puri in Bengal; Ramesvaram on the southern tip of India; Dwarka on the west coast; and Badrinath, 3,000 metres up in the Himalyas.

THE RIVER GANGES

The River Ganges is particularly sacred since it flows across India from its source in the Himalayas. Pilgrims visiting the holy city of Varanasi wash in the waters of the Ganges to receive a blessing from Shiva, lord of the universe. Varanasi is considered especially holy because it is located at the meeting point of two rivers – the Ganges and the Varuna. Anyone who dies here, murmuring the 'crossing-over' mantra, is assured of liberation and the cancelling of the consequences of karma.

opportunity for *darshan* – being in the presence of God; *murti* – 'seeing' the divine in the form of a temple image; and blessing.

Sacred places

Many parts of India are regarded as sacred by Hindus – indeed, for many Hindus, the whole country is believed to be holy. Special places can become very crowded at festival times, the most popular destinations being mountains, temples and rivers. The Himalayas are believed to be the god Himalaya, the father of Shiva's wife, Parvati. It is thought that Shiva himself sits in meditation on Mount Kailas.

For Hindus seven rivers are holy – the Indus, the Ganges, the Godavari, the Narmada, the Jumna, the Saraswati (which runs underground) and the Kaveri. Three of these rivers – the Ganges, the Narmada and the Kauveri – are treated as female deities. In a landscape that is so often barren and infertile, the rivers are worshipped as the bringers of life and energy.

Hinduism Today

There are over 800 million Hindus in the world today and sizeable Hindu communities in more than 160 countries. One in every six people in the modern world is a Hindu.

The spiritual home of Hinduism has always been India, where 85 per cent of all Hindus – some 650 million people – live. There were several Hindu reform movements during the 19th and 20th centuries which opposed the caste system and other forms of repression in the country. The most famous reformer was Mahatma Gandhi, who led India in a spiritual crusade against 'untouchability', the lowest level of caste, which reduced millions of Hindus to poverty.

Today, large Hindu communities are found in the West Indies and Africa as well as Sri Lanka, Guyana, Fiji and Bali. Some 800,000 Hindus live in the USA. Here there are many temples, including the Shiva-Vishnu temple in Livermore, California, where an attempt has been made to provide facilities for all the different strains of Hinduism found in the country. A resident team of priests seeks to meet the spiritual needs of the local Hindus. Small Hindu communities are also found throughout Europe with the largest outside Britain in the Netherlands where there are 160,000 adherents.

HINDUISM IN BRITAIN

The largest Hindu community outside India is found in Britain, where there are in excess of 1,200,000 people. Since the late 1960s Hindus have come to Britain mainly from Pakistan, Bangladesh, Sri Lanka, Indonesia, Guyana, the West Indies, Singapore, Malaysia and Uganda. They have tried to maintain their cultural and religious identity using their temples to ensure that the languages of Gujarati, Hindi and Punjabi continue to be spoken. Hindus believe that religion, cultural traditions and language are inseparably bound together – lose the language and the others will soon be lost as well.

The community is served by over 160 temples. The most spectacular opened in Neasden, London, on 20 August 1995. This building, with its carved domes, pinnacles and pillars, was built according to the teachings of the ancient Hindu scriptures, providing a new focus for Hindus in Britain and throughout Europe.

The exteriors of large Hindu temples are breathtaking in both their scale and the extent of their decoration. This temple is at Madras in India.

2,828 tons of limestone from Bulgaria and 2,000 tons of Carrara marble from Italy were used to build the temple in Neasden. These were shipped to India where it took 1,500 sculptors two years to carve each individual piece for the interior. All 26,300 individual pieces were numbered and brought to London for assembly.

Jewish history goes back about 4,000 years, making Judaism the oldest monotheistic religion, unless one counts Hinduism. Although the State of Israel was created in 1948 only 25 per cent of the world's Jews have returned to live there. The largest Jewish population is found in the USA, where 30 per cent of all Jews live.

Jews believe that they are the chosen people of God with a special part to play in the divine purpose. If you have a Jewish mother you are automatically born into the faith, although many Jews no longer keep up the old traditional religious practices. A key part of being a Jew is sharing a way of life – festivals,

Copies of the Torah are held aloft during a bar mitzvah festival at the Western Wall in Jerusalem.

food laws and rituals – even if the religious beliefs that underpin them are not universally shared.

Do not shelter yourself in any course of action by the idea that 'it is my affair'. It's your affair, but it is also mine and the community's. Nor can we neglect the world beyond. A fierce light beats upon the Jew. It's a grave responsibility this – to be a Jew; and you can't escape from it, even if you choose to ignore it.

C.G. MONTEFIORE, JEWISH LEADER

JUDAISM

Contents

Beginnings

Judaism looks back to Abraham as the father of the nation and to Moses who gave shape and form to its religious faith. Moses led the newly emergent nation from Egyptian slavery to the verge of the Promised Land.

Jewish history began with Abraham who heard God's call to settle in the land of Canaan. Abraham's grandson, Jacob, was promised many sons by God and from his 12 male offspring the tribes of Israel took their names. The word 'Jew' comes from the name of Israel's most powerful tribe, Judah.

Moses

When Moses was called by God, the Israelites were undergoing a debilitating time of slavery at the hands of the Egyptians. Moses heard the voice of God speaking to him

out of a burning bush that was not consumed by the fire and, at his command, Moses went to the Egyptian Pharaoh and demanded that the Israelites be freed. It was only after 10 plagues were visited on the Egyptians by God that his demand was met. The Israelites then spent 40 years travelling as nomads before they arrived at their Promised Land. It was during this journey – the exodus – that God gave the Ten Commandments to Moses on Mount Sinai. The Jews were also given many other laws to cover all aspects of their personal and social lives and these laws still govern the lives of Orthodox Jews today.

Judges and kings

After settling into the Promised Land of Canaan (later known as Palestine) the Israelites appointed a series of judges, including Gideon and Samson, to rule over them before they turned to a succession of kings. The first

> *Was Israel created for the sake of the Law, or the Law for the sake of Israel? Surely the Law for the sake of Israel. Now if the Law which was created for the sake of Israel will endure for ever, how much more will Israel which was created by the merit of the Law.*
>
> ECCLESIASTES RABBAH

At the annual Passover festival, held to commemorate the exodus of the Jews from slavery, a drop of wine is spilled for each of the 10 plagues. This reminds everyone that while the plagues brought freedom to the Jews they brought suffering for the Egyptians – so rejoicing must be tempered with sadness.

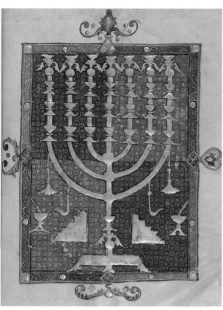

The seven-branched candlestick, or menorah, symbol of the modern State of Israel. An illustration for the Festival of Lights, or Hanukkah, from the *Hagadah*, which tells the story of the exodus.

Large numbers of Jews were taken into exile.

The Temple

The Temple was destroyed and rebuilt twice in the years that followed. The most thorough rebuilding was initiated by Herod the Great, but the task had hardly been completed, long after Herod's death, before the Romans finally demolished the Temple in 70 CE. It was never rebuilt and the Western Wall in Jerusalem is all that remains of this structure. The focus of Jewish faith moved from animal sacrifices in the Temple to the Torah, the rabbis who safeguarded Jewish tradition, and the synagogue as a place of learning and worship. The same emphasis remains today.

of these was Saul, who was succeeded by David and then David's son, Solomon. David was the best loved of Israel's kings and he wrote many of the Psalms in the Jewish Bible. Solomon built the Temple in Jerusalem, the beauty of which was fabled in the ancient world. After Solomon, though, a series of corrupt and mediocre kings brought the nation to its knees. Israel was divided, with the northern kingdom of Israel eventually falling to the Assyrians in 721 BCE, and the southern kingdom of Judah falling to the Babylonians in 586 BCE.

The Holocaust

Throughout history the Jews have been singled out by oppressors as the butt of their hatred and violence. Anti-Semitism reached its zenith with the Holocaust of the 20th century, when six million Jewish men, women and children were slaughtered by the Nazis.

No people in history has suffered like the Jews did in Europe in the 1930s and 1940s. Centuries of anti-Semitic poison exploded in the most frightening example of genocide in human history. In just six years, between 1939 and 1945, millions of Europeans were killed simply because they were Jews.

Concentration camps
The carnage in the German concentration camps of the Second World War was so horrific that it was called the Holocaust, which means 'burnt offering', although Jews prefer to call it the Shoah, meaning 'desolation'. Throughout Nazi-occupied Europe Jews were rounded up in vast numbers

The Yad Veshem memorial in Jerusalem, a vivid reminder of the Holocaust.

About a third of all Jews were murdered by the Nazis. At the end of the Holocaust just 11.5 million Jews remained worldwide. 250,000 of these lived in displaced persons' camps in Europe and 11.2 million were without a home. Some 650,000 of them went to live in the new State of Israel when it was established in 1948.

> *I wrote and I spoke as a lover of my country; as a convinced and public opponent of Hitler and the Nazis from the beginning... as one who abhors cruelty and barbarism such as Hitler and his followers practised for so long; and as a profound believer in the ideals of liberty and justice in defence of which Great Britain went to war.*
>
> BISHOP GEORGE BELL, OUTSPOKEN OPPONENT OF HITLER

and sent off to concentration camps to be gassed. There were 28 such camps and their names have become universal symbols of humankind's inhumanity to humankind – Dachau, Buchenwald, Auschwitz and Belsen among them. By 1944 more than 6,000 Jews a day were being executed at Auschwitz alone.

The Holocaust – an assessment

The Nazis claimed that the Jews represented everything that threatened the future of the German nation. Although Jews occupied many positions of power in Germany, and were very successful in business, they were said to be uncommitted to the future of the country. In a conflict of interests between religion and state, it was alleged that the main loyalty of the Jew was to God and not to the state, as the Nazis demanded. Moreover the Jews were held to be a threat to the the racial purity that Adolf Hitler was trying to achieve for the German people.

Only when the war ended did the world, and the Jewish people, become fully aware of what had happened. After being too shocked initially to respond, the Jewish community set about making sure that the world would never be allowed to forget. Days of memorial were arranged, special prayers were written and concentration camps were opened, untouched, to the public. A special memorial was built at Yad Veshem, in Jerusalem. The title itself means 'a place and a name'; the memorial is a bare room lit by a single candle with the names of all 28 concentration camps written on the floor. Also at Yad Veshem is a line of trees, called the 'Avenue of the Righteous', where each tree represents a Gentile who helped to save the life of a Jew during the Holocaust.

Scriptures

For devout Jews the Bible is central. Written in Hebrew, it has 39 books, just like the Christian Old Testament, but the books are in a different order.

Jews call their Bible the *TeNaKh* and it is comprised of three parts: the Law, or Torah, the Prophets, or *Nevi'im*, and the Writings, or *Ketuvim*.

The Torah

Jews often compare the Torah to the blueprint of the universe – it came before creation and before humanity. 'Torah' means 'law' or 'teaching' and refers to the totality of what is knowable about God and his relationship with the created world. In a narrower sense, however, it refers to the five books of Moses – Genesis, Exodus, Leviticus, Numbers and Deuteronomy – which come at the beginning of the Bible. Along with the Sabbath day the Torah is celebrated as God's greatest gift to the Jewish people.

An important part of Jewish worship is the reading aloud of set portions from the Torah. In the synagogue, passages from the Torah scroll, or *Sefer Torah*, are read on Sabbath mornings and afternoons, festival mornings and on Monday and Thursday mornings. It is considered a great honour, open only to men in the Orthodox tradition, to be asked to read from the Torah in public. The chosen person follows the passage in Hebrew using a *yad* – a hand-held pointer.

The Prophets

In the Jewish tradition there are eight books named after the prophets. The first four – Joshua, Judges, 1 and 2 Samuel and 1 and 2 Kings – are usually referred to as the Former

> *You taught your people the Torah and commandments; you instructed them in its statutes and its judgments, O our God, when we lie down as when we are awake, we shall always think and speak of your ordinances, and rejoice in the Torah and its commandments. It is your Torah that sustains us through life; on its teachings will we meditate day and night.*
> JEWISH PRAYER BOOK

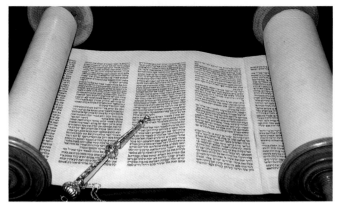

A scroll and a yad, for use in worship.

Prophets and are historical books. The other four are referred to as the Latter Prophets – Isaiah, Jeremiah, Ezekiel and the 12 Minor Prophets, which are considered to be one book. The Latter Prophets are largely collections of speeches delivered by the prophets, whose names the books bear, and collected together by their disciples. Prescribed selections from the prophetic books are read in the synagogue on Sabbaths, festivals and fast days.

THE TALMUD

For centuries an enormous number of judgments and opinions governing everyday religious, social and personal behaviour were kept alive in the Jewish community by word of mouth. In about 200 CE they were collected together in a document called the Mishnah. Soon the Mishnah itself was discussed and this new material was gathered together to form the Gemara, a commentary on the Mishnah. The Mishnah and Gemara together make up the Talmud. For centuries the Talmud has had considerable influence on the way that Jews have lived their lives.

The Writings

The Writings, the third section of the *TeNaKh*, are thought to be of less value than the other two, although they do contain the Psalms, which are regularly used in synagogue worship. Readings from the Writings are often given in the synagogue on festival days.

The Synagogue

The synagogue shows the public dimension of faith and comes after the home as the main focal point for Jewish religious life. The home is where most of the key rituals take place and emphasizes the personal side of faith.

During their Babylonian exile, in the sixth century BCE, Jews could no longer reach the Temple in Jerusalem so they met together in synagogues to study and pray. Many synagogue rituals were based on those of the Temple and the times of services reflected the pattern of Temple sacrifices. After the Romans destroyed the Jerusalem Temple in 70 CE it was never rebuilt, and Jewish religious life became centred on the synagogue instead.

The ark and its scrolls

The focal point of every synagogue is the ark which stands in front of the wall facing Jerusalem. This is an open cupboard covered by a

The synagogue is a place of learning, gathering, prayer and worship – a complete centre for the Jewish community. In Orthodox synagogues a minimum of 10 men – a *minyan* – needs to be present before prayer can be offered. An early-19th-century synagogue on the edge of Jerusalem.

heavy curtain. The ark reminds worshippers of the Holy of Holies, the 'inner sanctum', of the old Temple. This is where the original ark – the ark of the covenant – was kept. This held the stone tablets on which the Ten Commandments were written. Similarly, the ark in the synagogue contains the scrolls of the Torah – the *Sefer Torah*. Each of these scrolls has been hand-copied from the Torah in Hebrew and mounted on two wooden rollers ('trees of life'). They have silver heads and bells on the crown to represent God's sovereignty and they are wrapped in velvet with a breastplate to represent

The synagogue is the sanctuary of Israel. It was born out of Israel's longing for the living God. It has been to Israel throughout his endless wanderings a visible token of the presence of God in the midst of the people. It has shed a beauty which is the beauty of holiness and has ever stood on the high places as the champion of justice and brotherhood and peace. It is Israel's supreme gift to the world.

UNION PRAYER BOOK

that worn by the High Priest of Temple days. When a scroll becomes too old to use it is not destroyed, but buried like a human being.

During a synagogue service the scroll is taken out of the ark. Everyone stands up as it passes as a mark of respect for the central place the Torah has in Jewish life. It is a great honour to be asked to open and close the doors of the ark and to read from the *Sefer Torah* during Sabbath worship.

THE DAIS AND THE ETERNAL LIGHT

The reading desk in the synagogue stands on the dais, or *bimah*, and Torah readings are given from here. Traditionally the *bimah* is located in the centre of the synagogue, but in Progressive synagogues it stands in front of the ark. This means that the leader of the service either prays facing the ark (Orthodox) or facing the people (Progressive).

The 'eternal light', or *ner tamid*, burns above the ark, symbolizing God's eternal presence with his people as well as reminding worshippers of the seven-branched candlestick which was always alight in the Temple of old. Nearby two stone tablets on the wall represent the Ten Commandments.

The Sabbath Day

According to the Torah, God finished the work of creation after six days and, on the seventh day, he rested. The Sabbath day, or Shabbat, therefore, became a day of rest and relaxation for all Jews, and is enshrined in the Ten Commandments.

The Sabbath day is the weekly day of rest which begins at sunset on Friday and runs through until nightfall on Saturday. The Jewish scriptures give two reasons why all Jews should zealously guard the purity of this day:

◆ God himself rested on the seventh day after creating the world. Early rabbis formed the beautiful idea that rest from work is itself a creative act of God.

◆ After the Jewish exodus from Egyptian slavery, God instigated the Sabbath day so that everyone, including slaves and animals, had a day on which all work was prohibited.

> *Far more than Israel has kept the Sabbath, it is the Sabbath that has kept Israel.*
>
> AHAD HA'AM

According to the old rabbinic laws nothing can be carried on the Sabbath day outside the home. Sometimes, though, the problem is avoided by declaring a whole city to be a home if it has a wall or a fence around it. Jerusalem is one such city.

Apart from the Torah, Jews see the Sabbath day as God's greatest gift to them.

The Havdalah

The Sabbath day ends with a symbolic ceremony called the Havdalah, meaning 'separation'. A lit candle is extinguished in wine by the youngest member of the family while the mother or father passes a spice box, often in the shape of a tower, around for everyone to sniff. This reminds them of the sweetness of the Sabbath day as it draws to a close. The ceremony also makes a distinction between the Sabbath day and the week ahead.

Celebrating the Sabbath

The Sabbath day is the core celebration of Jewish life. It is the weekly reminder to all Jewish people of God's creation of life and of the covenant that he made with them. It provides leisure time for studying the Torah and enjoying prayer and worship. Traditional Jewish law, going back to the rabbis of old, bans all labour on this day and this is interpreted by devout Jews as including all business activity, spending of money, shopping, housework and use of any form of transport, electricity and even the telephone.

At home at least two candles are lit by the mother and children of a Jewish family before the Sabbath begins. The mother offers a prayer for the well-being of her husband and all her family. The mother's traditional hand-waving in front of the candles probably symbolizes the summoning of the Sabbath's spiritual light into the home.

The father then blesses his family. This is followed by a festive meal which unites all the family and is completed by the singing of special songs and the saying of grace.

On the Sabbath morning the whole family attends the synagogue. During the service seven people are called up to the *bimah* to follow the reader, who reads the prescribed portion from the Torah and offers a prayer thanking God for the gift of this unique day. Another person then reads a passage from the Prophets. The service ends with a sermon based on the Torah.

The Jewish Home

The home rather than the synagogue is the main focus of Jewish life. The house is considered to be sacred space, and the celebrations of more than one festival, including Passover, largely centre on the home.

A Jewish home is not simply a place to live but a house into which God has been invited. You can tell a Jewish home simply by looking at it – from the outside as well as from the inside.

The mezuzah

The Torah demands that a small parchment scroll in a container, a mezuzah, is attached to the upper third of all doorposts in the house, except those for the toilet, bathroom and garage. The mezuzah contains the words of the *Shema* (Deuteronomy 6:4–9). When entering or leaving their house or individual rooms Orthodox Jews kiss their fingertips before reaching up to touch the mezuzah, to show their love for God and the Torah.

Jews touch a mezuzah on entering and leaving a room. The mezuzah contains the *Shema*, and is the visible indication of a Jewish home.

Dietary laws

Meals in most Jewish homes are based on the dietary laws of *kashrut*. These stem from the laws given to Moses on Mount Sinai and recorded in the opening books of the Bible. They maintain that all vegetables, fruit, grains and nuts, and meat from animals that both chew the cud and have cloven hooves, are kosher to eat, as long as they have been prepared according to the rules of *shechita*. Meat and dairy foodstuffs must be prepared separately from each other, using utensils kept for these purposes alone.

In biblical times such laws preserved the uniqueness of the Jewish people and prevented close fellowship with other nations. The keeping of *kashrut* still helps to preserve a distinctive Jewish identity. It encourages self-discipline and obedience to God's law – even

The whole family tries to gather each week for the Sabbath meal. The challah, a white, leavened loaf of bread, is cut at a Sabbath meal.

Hear, O Israel: The Lord our God, the Lord is one. Love the Lord your God with all your heart and with all your soul and with all your strength. These commandments that I give you today are to be upon your hearts. Impress them on your children. Talk about them when you sit at home and when you walk along the road, when you lie down and when you get up. Tie them as symbols on your hands and bind them on your foreheads. Write them on the door-frames of your houses and on your gates.

THE *SHEMA*, DEUTERONOMY 6:4–9

though the reason for that obedience might not be immediately apparent.

The Jewish home, then, is a special place. Jewish tradition strongly emphasizes that it is a great act of kindness and love to provide hospitality, food and shelter for relatives, friends and strangers, especially those who are in the middle or at the end of a journey. It is a particularly great *mitzvah* ('good deed') to provide a Sabbath meal for those who would not otherwise be able to celebrate the holy day in an appropriate fashion.

Prayer

Prayer is the most important spiritual activity for every devout Jew. It is identified as a *mitzvah*, a duty or commandment, and one that Jews are expected to keep as part of their commitment to the covenant that God made with their ancestors.

Traditionally Jewish synagogues hold three services a day – in the morning, afternoon and evening – following the examples of Abraham, who prayed early in the morning; Isaac, who stopped his work to pray in the afternoon; and Jacob, who thanked God in the evening for his blessings. Orthodox Jews coming together to pray in the synagogue must form a *minyan* – a quorum of 10 adult males – but this rule has been abolished in Reform and Progressive synagogues.

> *Great is the sanctity of tefillin for as long as the tefillin are upon man's head and arm, he is humble and God-fearing and is not drawn after frivolity and idle talk, and does not have evil thoughts, but directs his heart to words of truth and righteousness. Therefore a man should try to have them on all day... Even though they should be worn all day it is a greater obligation to wear them during prayer.*
>
> MOSES MAIMONIDES,
> 12TH-CENTURY JEWISH
> PHILOSOPHER

The symbols of prayer

A key feature of Jewish prayer is the value attached to different symbols. Three are particularly significant:

◆ The *tallit* is the robe in which a worshipper wraps himself during prayer. This garment has fringes attached to each of its four corners, in keeping with the instructions found in Numbers 15:37–41.

Men wear the *tallit* at morning prayer only, draping it across their backs.

◆ The phylacteries, or *tefillin*, are cube-shaped leather boxes containing four passages from the scriptures, which are attached to the head and left arm and, like the *tallit*, worn during morning prayer. The *tefillin* are not worn on the Sabbath or festival days. In Progressive synagogues women

JEWISH PRAYERS

The *Siddur* is the Jewish prayer book. The most important prayers in Jewish worship are the *Shema* (Deuteronomy 6:4–9), which is the nearest that Jews come to having a statement of belief; the *Amidah*, 18 blessings at the heart of Jewish worship; the *Aleinu*, which praises God and prays for Israel and the world; and the *Kaddish*, a prayer for holiness often used in times of mourning.

often wear the *tallit* and *tefillin* as well as men, but not in Orthodox synagogues.

◆ The yarmulke is the skullcap worn by Jewish men. It is believed that studying or praying bareheaded shows a marked disrespect for God. The most obedient wear the yarmulke at all times, but the majority only wear it while praying.

A man wearing his prayer shawl, or *tallit*, and phylacteries, or *tefillin*, for prayer. The phylacteries are strapped to the head and left arm and contain verses of scripture.

Circumcision and Coming of Age

Jews share the rite of circumcision with Muslims, although it is carried out for very different reasons. The popular coming-of-age ceremony of bar mitzvah is comparatively modern and signifies the transition from boyhood to manhood.

Circumcision, or *brit milah*, of a male child on the eighth day after birth is the oldest Jewish custom still practised today. God gave it to Abram as a 'sign of the covenant' between them. It is not a token of induction into the Jewish faith – that's brought about by being born to a Jewish mother – but a physical sign of a child sharing in the timeless covenant of God.

Traditionally circumcision (removing the foreskin of the penis) was performed by the boy's father, but now it is usually carried out by a trained Jewish circumciser, or *mohel*, in the baby's home or in the synagogue. Orthodox tradition calls for 10 males to be present while the rite is performed. The godmother carries the child into the gathering, where he is held by the godfather, but

A Jewish boy celebrates his bar mitzvah by the Western Wall in Jerusalem.

> *Blessed are You, O Lord our God, ruling Spirit of the Universe, who has commanded us to enter into the Covenant of our father Abraham.*
>
> FATHER'S BLESSING
> AT CIRCUMCISION

the mother is not present, in accordance with tradition. Afterwards, the boy receives his name before a drop of wine is placed on his lips. The father drinks the rest. The family prays that the child will grow up to love God, study the Torah and live a life of good deeds.

Coming of age

The Talmud instructs that 'as soon as a child can speak, his father teaches him Torah'. As well as learning the Hebrew language he's also taught the *Shema* and the Ten Commandments. Then, on his 13th birthday, he becomes a bar mitzvah, a 'son of the commandment', and from this time on Jewish tradition insists that he's old enough to carry out all of his religious obligations.

On the first Sabbath day after his 13th birthday the boy, wearing his *tallit* and *tefillin*, is called up to the *bimah* to read the prescribed passage from the *Sefer Torah* in Hebrew. He can then be called on to read the Torah at any time and he can be accepted as part of the *minyan* which makes any public act of prayer legitimate.

BAT HAYIL AND BAT MITZVAH

A girl celebrates her bat mitzvah in a Reform synagogue.

In recent years, girls brought up in Orthodox synagogues have been given the opportunity to become *bat hayils* – 'daughters of valour'. This takes place near their 12th birthdays. Reform and Progressive synagogues, however, have ceremonies which are much closer to bar mitzvah. These are called bat mitzvah – meaning 'daughter of the commandment'. After this the girl will be permitted to read a passage in Hebrew from the Torah, although she may be given a passage from the Prophets or the Writings instead.

Marriage and Death

Jewish home life is centred on the sacred nature of marriage, and death is a very unwelcome intruder into that home. Jews do not hold very clear beliefs about life after death.

In Jewish tradition marriage is held up as the ideal state for everyone. Although the prime motive for marriage is to create the ideal environment for children it is also, in the words of one marriage blessing, 'to give joy and gladness, mirth and exultation, pleasure and delight, love, peace and friendship' to the couple.

The wedding service

Marriage services are essentially the same across all Jewish traditions. Synagogue marriages, however, must be between a Jewish man and a Jewish woman. They cannot be carried out on the Sabbath day or any other festival day. The service begins with the signing of the wedding document – the *ketubah* – which sets out the man's responsibilities but does not contain any promises from the woman. The ceremony is carried out under the wedding canopy, the *chuppah*, to symbolize the home the couple are setting up together. The couple share a glass of wine during the service

> *Let the glory of God be extolled, let his great name be exalted in the world whose creation he willed. May his kingdom prevail, in our own day, in our own lives, and the life of all Israel. Let us say, Amen... May the source of peace send peace to all who mourn and comfort to all who are bereaved. Amen.*
>
> KADDISH PRAYER

After the marriage ceremony the couple are led to a quiet room where the marriage can be consummated. Only after this can the traditional wedding feast take place.

to symbolize their common destiny. It is ended by the groom breaking a wineglass under his feet, to remind everyone of the Jerusalem Temple's destruction in 70 CE.

Death

Jews look upon life as a gift from God and death as a sad, but inevitable, conclusion to a life well lived. The rabbi is not expected to be present as a person's life draws to a close since that's the responsibility of the *chevra kadishah* – a group of men and women in the synagogue noted for their holiness. They stay with a dying person until the end and then look after the corpse until burial – a great honour in the Jewish community. This voluntary act of love shown to the dying is a true *mitzvah* since

During a Jewish wedding the couple stand under the chuppah, a canopy which symbolizes the home they will make together.

it is carried out without any thought of reward.

A Jewish man's body is wrapped in the *tallit* he's prayed in since his bar mitzvah, then placed in a simple wooden coffin so that his head rests on the earth from the Holy Land which has been placed inside it. During the funeral service, which takes place within 24 hours of death, the rabbi gives a eulogy, psalms are chanted and the Kaddish prayer is recited.

As the body is carried to the grave the pallbearers stop seven times as a reminder of the seven vanities listed in the book of Ecclesiastes. As the coffin is lowered into the grave, members of the immediate family, followed by other mourners, shovel earth on top. This is to encourage the living to look to the future – very much the emphasis of the Jewish faith. As the Talmud teaches, the dead person has now begun his or her journey to eternity. The strict rules governing mourning are designed to help the living return to a normal life in as ordered a way as possible.

The Jewish Year

Many festivals and holy days are celebrated in the Jewish year. Some of them, such as New Year and the Day of Atonement, are extremely serious while others, like the festival of lights and Purim, are much more celebratory.

A year consists of 12 months based on the lunar cycle. According to tradition the numbering of the years is calculated from creation in 3760 BCE.

New Year and the Day of Atonement

New Year (Rosh Hashanah) and the Day of Atonement (Yom Kippur) begin the Jewish year. Tradition teaches that on Rosh Hashanah three books are opened in heaven. The first lists all who are righteous and to be rewarded for their good deeds; the third reveals the wicked whom God will punish; while the second contains those who have the 10 days between Rosh Hashanah and Yom Kippur to show they are worthy of heaven. At Yom Kippur Jews meet with God through 25 hours of fasting in the synagogue, seeking divine forgiveness.

Festivals of shelters and 'rejoicing in the law'

During the festival of Sukkot Jewish people build tabernacles, open to the sky, in their homes and synagogues. They spend time in the tabernacles with their families as they remember

> The Lord said to Moses, 'Say to the Israelites: "On the first day of the seventh month you are to have a day of rest, a sacred assembly commemorated with trumpet blasts. Do no regular work, but present an offering made to the Lord by fire… The tenth day of this seventh month is the Day of Atonement. Hold a sacred assembly and deny yourselves, and present an offering made to the Lord by fire. Do no work on that day.'"
>
> LEVITICUS 23:23–25, 27–28

the goodness of God in creation.

Simchat Torah (the 'rejoicing in the law') starts as Sukkot ends. The cycle of Torah readings in the synagogue is now complete and another begins. Not a breath is taken as one passes over into the other, expressing the strong belief that the Torah is eternal, without beginning or end. The one who reads the final passage of the old cycle, Deuteronomy 33 and 34, is called the *Hatan*

Rosh Hashanah and Yom Kippur are ushered in with the sound of a ram's-horn trumpet, or shofar.

PURIM AND SHAVUOT

Purim, a minor late-winter festival, celebrates events recorded in the book of Esther, wherein the Jewish queen of Persia, Esther, manages to foil the plans of Haman to wipe out the whole Jewish community. During this festival the book of Esther, or *megillah* ('scroll'), is read in the synagogue amid wild celebrations.

The festival of Shavuot commemorates when God gave the law to Moses on Mount Sinai. Shavuot is also known as Pentecost since it occurs 50 days after Pesach (Passover).

Torah – the 'bridegroom of the Torah' – to illustrate that Jews are 'married' to the Torah.

Festival of Lights

The Festival of Lights, or Hanukkah, is celebrated over eight days in December and is the only festival not mentioned in the Jewish scriptures. It is based on a legend from the second century BCE when a small army of Jewish soldiers won an unlikely victory over the Seleucid king, Antiochus IV. Hanukkah celebrates how the menorah, the Temple's seven-branched candlestick, stayed alight for eight days, although it only had enough oil for one.

Passover

Passover, or Pesach, celebrates an event which has no equal in Jewish history – the exodus from slavery in Egypt. Jews see this as a glorious demonstration of God's power as well as a reiteration of the covenant he had made with Abraham and his offspring.

Pesach, a spring festival, lasts for eight days among Jews of the Diaspora (those who have been dispersed throughout the world) but it is a day shorter in Israel and among Reform Jews. The word 'Pesach' comes from the paschal lamb which was offered to God as a sacrifice on the eve of the festival in the old Temple. The name 'Passover' derives from the story of the angel of death 'passing over' the Israelites' houses in the last of the 10 plagues, the decisive act of God which finally persuaded the Egyptians to release their captives.

The Seder meal

Before Pesach begins, the house is thoroughly cleaned and searched for any traces of leavened bread – *hametz*. This is turned into a children's game in which pieces of bread are deliberately planted. Then the whole family eats a special Seder ('order') meal which follows a traditional pattern laid down in the *Hagadah*, a book telling the story of the exodus.

During the meal those present drink four glasses of wine, recalling the promises God made to Moses. A fifth glass remains untouched on the table, demonstrating the belief that, at some future time, the prophet Elijah will return to earth at Passover to herald the beginning of the Messiah's reign on earth. The youngest child then asks four standard questions and the head of the household tells the story of the exodus in answering them.

A special plate on the table holds six dishes that remind

> *In the first month, on the 14th day of the month in the evening, is the Lord's passover. And on the 15th day of the same month is the feast of unleavened bread to the Lord; seven days you shall eat unleavened bread.*
> LEVITICUS 23:4–8

By the time Pesach begins there must be no *hametz* (leavened bread) in the house. Even special crockery and cutlery is used at Pesach, and no other time, to make sure that there are no traces of *hametz*.

everyone of the exodus. Two of them, a roasted shankbone and an egg, are not eaten but all the others are tasted:

◆ Three matzah loaves symbolize the fact that when the Jews left Egypt they were in such a hurry they could not wait for their bread to rise, so took only unleavened bread with them. They eat just unleavened bread throughout Pesach.

◆ Bitter herbs, or *Maror*, recall the bitterness of over 400 years of slavery in Egypt.
◆ Parsley dipped in salt water or vinegar is a reminder of the tears of the Hebrew slaves.
◆ *Haroset* – a mixture of nuts, wine and apple – symbolizes the cement that Jews were forced to use to build houses for the Egyptians.

A vital element of the Passover is sharing blessings with others, so the less fortunate are invited to the meal as guests. Special synagogue services are also held to mark the festival. Here the Torah is read, the story of the exodus is recounted and psalms of praise are chanted.

A stained-glass window commemorating the Passover festival.

Types of Judaism

Judaism today is more divided than at any other time in its history. It is not uncommon for some towns to have several synagogues each offering their own version of 'true Judaism'. Sometimes these differences have led to acrimonious debate and even violence, especially in Israel.

There are five major types of Judaism: Orthodox Judaism, Conservative Judaism, Reconstructionism, Hasidic Judaism and Reform Judaism.

Orthodox Judaism

Orthodox Jews are the traditional followers of rabbinic Judaism who see themselves as the only faithful upholders of the unchanging faith of Israel. Orthodox Judaism lays full emphasis on the authenticity of the revelations in the Bible, especially the Torah, and the full authority of the rabbinic law and its interpretations in the Talmud. Orthodox Jews today are obliged to keep the 613 commandments, or *mitzvot*, of the Torah. At one end of the Orthodox spectrum are the Ultra-Orthodox – literally those who tremble in fear at God and his law. At the other end are the Modern Orthodox, who follow the teaching of Samuel Raphael Hirsch (1808–88), a German rabbi and religious thinker, and believe in a synthesis between the Torah and Western learning.

A woman rabbi reads from the Torah in a Reform service.

> *Reform declared that Judaism has changed throughout time and that Jewish law is no longer binding. Orthodoxy denies both propositions, insisting on the binding character of Jewish law and negating the view that Judaism has evolved. Conservative Judaism agrees with Orthodoxy in maintaining the authority of Jewish law and with Reform in that Judaism grew and evolved through time.*
>
> RABBI ROBERT GORDIS

Conservative Judaism

Conservative Judaism began in the 1940s and has clung to almost all the traditions of the faith while making some concessions to reform. Conservative Judaism is the dominant force among American Jewry.

Reconstructionism

Founded in the USA in the 1920s by Rabbi Mordecai Kaplan who, although from an Orthodox background, outlined a vision of Judaism more concerned with the culture than the beliefs and practices of the Jews. Kaplan rejected the idea of an omniscient God who made a covenant with the Jews through Abraham and gave his chosen people the eternal laws in the Torah.

Hasidic Judaism

Begun in the 1700s by Baal Shem Tov (1700–60), Hasidism moved away from the Orthodox emphasis upon the scholarly and concentrated instead on the spiritual and mystical traditions of Judaism. Hasidic leaders (*rebbe*) are those believed to have specific spiritual gifts over and above those granted to the rabbi. Hasidic movements are particularly strong today in Israel and the USA.

Reform Judaism

Reform Judaism began in 1840s' Germany and taught that all Jews have responsibilities to the country in which they live as well as to the Jewish faith. This led Reform Jews to distinguish between those elements of Judaism which have lasting value and those which are temporary. Jewish tradition, they argue, needs to be reinterpreted in the light of what is acceptable today. For instance, Reform synagogues do not separate men and women in worship, they have an equivalent service to bar mitzvah for girls and they ordain women rabbis.

Judaism Today

No religion has emerged untouched from the 20th century but none has been more affected by events beyond its control than Judaism. Over 30 per cent of the world's Jews died during the Second World War, a blow from which Judaism has not yet recovered and probably never will.

Small Jewish communities exist in almost every country of the world. In the early 20th century the two major centres of the world's Jewry were Eastern Europe, especially Poland and Russia, and the USA. During the Second World War, Eastern European Jewry was decimated by the Nazis occupying Hungary, Poland, Czechoslovakia and the Baltic States. The deaths of six million Jewish men, women and children persuaded the world that a Jewish State was needed. The creation of Israel in 1948 meant the Jews at last had a home of their own. By the year 2000, 4,700,000 of the world's Jews lived there.

Jews in the USA

The largest community of Jews (5,900,000) is still found in the USA. This community exercises a considerable influence in American affairs, particularly in business and political matters. At the same

> *Migration is an unsettling business. Jews are no strangers to migration; in fact it is a deeply rooted feature of the Jewish historical experience. But that knowledge does not make the anxieties and practical difficulties easier to cope with… There is a period of uncertainty and of adjustment which may last over several generations: there are problems of acceptance in a new society, and a certain nostalgia for a lost past.*
> NICHOLAS DE LANGE

time the American Jewish community has experienced similar problems to Jewish communities elsewhere. The synagogue is less influential than it used to be with fewer than 50 per cent of Jews now affiliated to a place of worship. More and more American Jews have been 'assimilated' into a secular culture with the figures for mixed marriages climbing

The main feature of a synagogue service is the reading of the Torah. The Torah scroll, or *Sefer Torah*, is housed in the ark, a cupboard located in the wall of the synagogue, facing Jerusalem.

steeply. In the 1950s fewer than seven per cent of Jews married outside the faith but the figure is now well above 40 per cent and still rising. As fewer than half of the children of mixed marriages remain in the Jewish faith, the future for the community looks gloomy.

Judaism elsewhere

Conflict between the Israelis and their Arab neighbours is long-standing and is, as yet, unresolved. Jews from North Africa and the Arab states have emigrated to Israel in large numbers, and the country has largely become a mixture of Ashkenazim – Eastern European Jews, many of whom are descended from Holocaust survivors – and Sephardim – Jews from the old Islamic empire. Large numbers of Jews from Yemen and Falashas from Ethiopia were welcomed to Israel after civil wars broke out in their homelands. During the Cold War small groups of Jews were allowed out of Russia to emigrate to Israel but, after the collapse of the Soviet empire, this trickle swelled into a flood.

Large Jewish communities are also found in other parts of the world. The Jewish community in Britain numbers some 300,000, while there are 95,000 Jews in Australia, 98,000 in South Africa, 356,000 in Canada and 225,000 in Argentina.

People have followed the teachings of the Buddha for more than 2,500 years – from India, where he lived, to Europe and America, where the faith is strong. There are almost 400 million Buddhists worldwide.

Buddhists believe that human beings are tied into the cycle of birth, life and death through desire and that they can be born countless times at different levels of existence. They also believe that it is possible to escape from successive rebirths and so reach nirvana. The teachings of the Buddha are a guide for all Buddhists who are anxious to develop the qualities of nonviolence, wisdom and compassion. Eventually they, like the Buddha and others, will be enlightened.

Buddhists believe in an ultimate reality but they do not call this reality 'God'. Many Buddhists feel happier

Part of the collection of 394 gilded images of the Buddha at Wat Po, Bangkok, Thailand.

to talk in terms of a 'philosophy of life' rather than a religion.

Buddhism offers a way of intelligent reflection on the human predicament. We all experience being born in the human form and having to... experience all kinds of things, from the best to the worst, from pleasure to pain... There is no one exempt from this experience of suffering, of growth, of ageing, of death...
VENERABLE SUMEDHO

BUDDHISM

Contents

The Buddha

The highly privileged palace life of Prince Siddharta Gautama was changed for ever when he saw an old man, a sick man, a group of mourners and a holy man for the first time. After years of searching he found the answer to the problem of suffering.

Siddharta Gautama was born about 560 BCE in north-eastern India, one of the world's greatest intellectual and spiritual centres. A legend attached to his birth suggests that Maya, his mother, dreamed a white elephant entered her womb. Ten months later she gave birth as the earth trembled during a full moon in May. Maya died seven days later because, as the legend says, she who has borne a Buddha cannot serve any other purpose. The child was brought up in the greatest luxury by his aunt.

Rahula

The young prince married Gopa, or Yashodara, and he called their first son Rahula, meaning 'chains', because he felt imprisoned by his lifestyle. When he managed to creep out of the palace four experiences reinforced this:

◆ He saw a frail old man and witnessed how old age destroys memory, beauty and strength.

He had not encountered old age before.

◆ He saw an invalid racked with pain; he was shocked to see such suffering and 'trembled like the reflection of the moon on rippling water'. He had not encountered suffering before.

◆ He saw weeping mourners with a funeral procession and was disturbed by the distress of death. He had not encountered death before.

◆ He saw a wandering holy man, contented and joyful, travelling around with an alms bowl. He suddenly understood that all of life's pleasures were

When Siddharta Gautama was very young a Hindu Brahmin prophesied that he would become an enlightened being who would help others to overcome suffering in their lives. Eight more Brahmins confirmed this.

> Then as the third watch drew on he thought: 'Alas, all living things wear themselves out. Over and over again they are born, they age and die, pass on to a new life, and are reborn. What is more, greed and false hopes blind them and they are blind from birth. Frightened, they do not yet know how to get out of this great ill.' Siddharta found that lack of self-knowledge was the key.
>
> BUDDHIST SCRIPTURES

worthless. What he longed for now was true knowledge, so he left his palace in the middle of the night to find it.

The enlightened Buddha. Siddharta Gautama's reaction to seeing suffering was to begin searching for the meaning of life. After five years of strict asceticism he passed through three stages of enlightenment and became the Buddha.

Enlightenment

Siddharta joined many other holy men in seeking true knowledge. First he tried yoga exercises. Then he lived in extreme poverty for five years with five companions. Yet no answer came. He sat in isolation under a *bodhi* tree to meditate.

Then it happened. During the next three nights he went through three stages of enlightenment, resisting the temptations of Mara, the evil one. On the first night all of his previous lives passed before him. On the second night he saw the cycle of birth, life and death – and the law that governs it. On the third night he came to understand the Four Noble Truths: the universality of suffering, the origin of suffering (human desire), the cure for suffering and the way to find that cure. He realized that all people suffer; suffering stems from human craving and if the craving ceases the suffering stops. Thus he became the Buddha – the 'enlightened one'.

After this, Siddharta was asked three times by the high God, Brahma, to help others towards enlightenment. This he did for the next 44 years, and his first followers were his five companions in poverty.

Forms of Buddhism

In the centuries after the Buddha's death Theravada and Mahayana Buddhism emerged as the two main schools of Buddhist thought.

Theravada Buddhism (the lesser vehicle) is the way to salvation usually followed by monks. Mahayana Buddhism is the largest of the two schools with over 300 million followers worldwide.

Theravada Buddhism

Theravada Buddhism is practised in Sri Lanka, Myanmar (formerly Burma), Thailand and other parts of South-East Asia. 'Theravada' means 'the way of the elders'. Its teachings are based on scriptures called the *Pali Canon*, which Theravada Buddhists believe to be the most accurate record of what the Buddha said and did. Above all, the *Pali Canon* emphasizes that the Buddha was only a man, one in a succession of buddhas, and that enlightenment can be reached by following his example and teachings.

In the Theravada community there are two groups of people:

◆ The monks and nuns, or *bhikkus*, who are totally dependent on lay Buddhists for

Buddhist monks on their early-morning alms round in a village in Myanmar (formerly Burma).

ZEN BUDDHISM

Of the many types of Buddhism in Japan, Zen Buddhism has to be one of the most unusual. It teaches that a person must get beyond words to understand existence. A monk may spend a lifetime meditating on a single sentence or word called a koan. A koan is a puzzle which has no answer, a popular one being, 'What is the sound of one hand clapping?' Zen Buddhists often create beautiful gardens as an aid to meditation.

their food and clothing, are free of domestic duties so stand the best chance of reaching nirvana. Closest of all to enlightenment are the 'forest monks', who practise a very strict form of meditation. It is almost impossible for a layperson to achieve enlightenment, so anyone serious about reaching it must become a monk or a nun – a *bhikku*.

◆ Householders achieve merit for a future rebirth by making offerings of food, clothes and money to the monks and nuns.

Mahayana Buddhism

'Mahayana' means 'the great vehicle' and Mahayana Buddhists view Siddharta Gautama as superhuman. They also believe that there have existed, do exist and will exist many other buddhas. Mahayana Buddhism claims to offer more possibilities for enlightenment than Theravada Buddhism. These are based on three principles which are thought to be in keeping with the Buddha's teachings:

◆ People do not have to rely on their own efforts to reach nirvana. Instead, they are helped towards enlightenment by Bodhisattvas – people who have reached enlightenment but remain on earth by choice in order to help others towards nirvana.

◆ Anything can be used as a vehicle in the journey towards enlightenment – including mantras, koans, wood-cutting or water-drawing.

◆ The *Sangha* can help those who wish to reach enlightenment. The *Sangha* is the community of monks and nuns who follow the Buddha's teachings.

Mahayana Buddhism is subdivided into many other schools and is the main form of Buddhism found in Japan, Korea, Mongolia, China, Tibet and Nepal.

Scriptures

As a skilled teacher, the Buddha used parables, illustrations from nature, similes, metaphors, questions and answers, discussion and debate to convey his message – yet he did not write anything down. After his death his disciples began to gather fragments of his teaching together.

Buddhist writings fall into two main groups: those which tradition teaches have come from Buddha himself and the writings of various holy men and scholars. Both Theravada and Mahayana Buddhism have their own scriptures.

Theravada scriptures
For many centuries the early teachings of the Buddha were kept alive and passed down orally by the *Sangha*, the community of Buddhist monks and nuns. In the first century BCE these teachings were written in the language of Pali on palm-leaf manuscripts in Sri Lanka. The Buddha himself would have spoken a dialect of Pali. These scriptures are known as the *Pali Canon*. This falls into three sections called the *Tipitaka* (the 'three baskets'):

◆ The *Vinaya Pitaka* is concerned with the *Sangha*.

> *To be attached to a certain view and to look down on other views as inferior – this the wise man calls a fetter.*
>
> SUTTA NIPATA

◆ The *Sutta Pitaka* consists of various discourses given by the Buddha.
◆ The *Abhimdhamma Pitaka* is made up of analyses of the Buddha's teachings.

These scriptures are still read in their original language where possible, although the use of a translation is perfectly acceptable.

Mahayana scriptures
The earliest Mahayana scriptures were written in Sanskrit, an early Indian language. Much of their content is found in the *Pali Canon* but other books have been added. It is claimed that these additional works are

authoritative as the 'Buddha word'. One of the most famous of these is the *Vimalakirti Sutra*, which is about a householder who is more holy than all the Bodhisattvas.

Tibetan Buddhists believe that many scriptures were hidden until the Buddhist community was ready to receive, and understand, their teachings. Such scriptures are still being discovered today, the most widely used being the *Tibetan Book of the Dead*.

Novice monks in a monastery at Myanmar (formerly Burma) study the scriptures. There is no universally recognized canon, but different traditions of Buddhism revere their own collections of writings.

Beliefs

After the Buddha reached enlightenment he decided to forgo immediate entry into nirvana in order to teach his vision to others. This vision lies in understanding the Four Noble Truths and following the Eightfold Path (the Middle Way).

The Four Noble Truths and the Eightfold Path lie at the heart of the Buddha's teachings. Eightfold Path, or Middle Way, between the extremes of asceticism and sensuality.

The Four Noble Truths

All Buddhist practice is designed to help people reach a full understanding of the Four Noble Truths, which are the foundation for all Buddhist belief:

◆ All life involves suffering. Buddhist teaching aims to help people understand and overcome it.
◆ The cause of suffering is a craving for life, pleasure and money.
◆ Eliminating the craving means the suffering will also be eliminated.
◆ The Middle Way between asceticism and hedonism is the only way to remove this craving.

By eliminating selfish desire and attachment to this world, the cycle of birth, life and death can be finally broken. This is achieved by following the

The Eightfold Path

The Buddha gave his followers several 'pictures' to help them understand this path – the Middle Way. He compared it to a tank of water for those who are thirsty; a fire to warm up those suffering from the cold; a garment to cover those who are naked; and a lamp for those who are surrounded by darkness. The different steps along the Eightfold Path are rather like the spokes of a wheel: although

One of the Buddha's titles is *Tathagata* ('gone thus') and in following the Middle Way each Buddhist is following the Buddha towards enlightenment.

> *This, O Bhikkus, is the Noble Truth of Suffering: death is suffering; presence of objects we hate is suffering; separation from objects we love is suffering; not to obtain what we desire is suffering. Briefly, the fivefold clinging to existence is suffering. All existence is dukkha [suffering].*
>
> THE BUDDHA

The Buddha's teachings explain the nature of suffering and how to escape from it, and from the endless cycle of birth, death and rebirth, by reaching a state of nirvana. Everything in life is governed by karma – the law of cause and effect. So a morally good life generates positive karma in the next life. But the ultimate aim is to reach nirvana and be completely released from the law of karma.

they each have value of their own they gain real strength from their unity with each other The eight 'spokes' are:

◆ right understanding of the Four Noble Truths.
◆ right thoughts, leading to love towards all living forms, even the most humble.
◆ right speech, which must be pure, noble and well intentioned.
◆ right action, involving moral behaviour, being considerate to others and showing kindness to all living creatures.
◆ right livelihood, meaning a Buddhist must not earn a living from anything that

involves violence or from following their religion; Buddhist monks must be kept by the community.
◆ right effort to banish all evil thoughts.
◆ right mindfulness, involving constant awareness of the needs of others.
◆ right concentration using meditation, which allows a person to become inwardly calm and at peace with themselves and the world.

Teachings

A number of other teachings were added later to the
Four Noble Truths and the Eightfold Path. The most
important are the Five Precepts.

The cycle of birth, life and
death means nothing in
existence is permanent and
everything is in a state of
constant flux. This is known as
anicca, meaning 'impermanence'.
When human beings strive for
permanence the outcome is
suffering, or *dukkha*. Buddha
taught that, as everything human

is constantly changing, all
experience involves suffering and
there is no permanent self which
remains unchanged. In this
respect Hinduism and Buddhism
are different. Hinduism teaches
that there is a permanent soul,
the atman, which survives death
and is reborn. Buddha, however,
taught that the 'soul' is no more

The Wheel of
Life turned by
Yama, the lord
of the dead. The
central circle
represents
greed, hatred
and delusion.
Moving
outwards, the
next circle shows
various spheres
of existence,
from the realm
of hell to the
realm of the
gods. The
outermost circle
shows the chain
of karma. The
whole cycle is
continually
repeated.

Most Buddhists are vegetarians and pacifists.

than a bundle of experiences which evaporates at death.

The Five Precepts

The Five Precepts are moral guidelines which all Buddhists try to follow:

◆ They avoid taking life or harming any living thing.
◆ They avoid taking that which is not given.
◆ They avoid all sexual misconduct.
◆ They avoid all unworthy speech, such as lying, rumour-spreading and gossip.
◆ They avoid any contact with drugs and alcohol, since these cloud the mind and judgment.

Nirvana

The never-ending cycle of birth, life and death is called samsara, meaning 'endless wandering'. All living things are part of this cycle and they cannot be released from it until they reach nirvana. Nirvana, the 'place of coolness', is the state in which the flames of passion and greed have been extinguished.

> It [the Dharma] is like a man, Bhikkus, who as he is going on a journey should see a great stretch of water... but there may be neither a boat for crossing over, nor a bridge across... It occurs to him that in order to cross over... he should fashion a raft out of grass and sticks... When he has done this and has crossed over it occurs to him that the raft has been very useful and he wonders if he ought to proceed taking it with him... What do you think, monks?
>
> THE BUDDHA

KARMA AND REINCARNATION

The sum of human actions, or karma, has a direct influence on the shape of a person's future existence. The extent of moral actions determines whether a person is reincarnated or has reached nirvana. Lay Buddhists try to build up good karma by performing commendable deeds. In this way they can hope for a good rebirth. Apart from understanding the Four Noble Truths and following the Eightfold Path, Buddhists also try to store up merit by supporting their local monks. As the monks are not allowed to earn any money they are dependent for their food and clothing on the local Buddhist community. Lay Buddhists often sponsor the ordination of monks as well as placing food, and other gifts, in their begging bowls. The monks are only allowed to beg before midday.

Worship

The Buddha was a teacher, not a god. Buddhist worship – whether in a monastery, a temple or the home – involves paying homage before the statue of the Buddha and reciting sacred prayers.

The monastery, or vihara, is the key centre of Buddhist devotion, although worship also takes place in the temple and in the shrine room of a Buddhist home.

The monastery

The monastery is a place for spiritual activity as well as learning and study. Here the monks follow a life of devotion and meditation – the secrets of which they are expected to pass on to lay Buddhists. They teach the Dharma – 'universal law', the Buddha's teachings – to the people and try to meet their spiritual needs. Monks are also involved in key life ceremonies, especially those of birth, marriage and death.

Buddhist monks live according to the guidelines in the *Pali Canon*. They also observe the Five Precepts, to which are added five further rules:

◆ They are not allowed to participate in any form of entertainment, including singing and dancing.

◆ They cannot go to sleep on a luxurious bed.
◆ They cannot eat at times outside the monastic timetable.
◆ They cannot use perfumes or deodorants.
◆ They must not accept any gifts of gold or silver.

The act of worship

The body, language and thoughts are integral elements in Buddhist worship, so silent meditation, teaching, the making of offerings and chanting are all involved. Before entering the shrine room, which contains images of the Buddha, worshippers remove their shoes. They then place their hands together before prostrating themselves in either a kneeling

I make the offering to the Buddha with these flowers and through this merit may there be release. Even as these flowers must fade so my body goes towards destruction. To him of fragrant body and face, fragrant with infinite values, to the Buddha I make offering with fragrant incense.
BUDDHIST PRAYER

The temple of the Sera Monastery near Lhasa, Tibet. Life in Tibet was closely bound up with the monastic tradition until the closure of the monasteries by the Chinese authorities, which began in the 1950s.

position, for Theravada Buddhists, or a standing position, for Tibetan Buddhists. Three basic offerings can be made:

◆ Flowers are offered as a reminder of the impermanence of life.
◆ Light is offered to dispel the darkness.
◆ Incense is offered as a reminder of the lasting fragrance of the Buddha's teaching.

Mahayana Buddhists make a sevenfold offering to the Buddha, which is often symbolized by seven bowls of water that can be used for drinking, bathing or foot-washing.

Finally, after the offering has been made, the Three Refuges – the Buddha, the Dharma and the *Sangha* – and the Five Precepts are recited. Some mantras are then chanted and there is a period of silent meditation. Usually there is also some teaching before worship ends.

Prayer and Meditation

Buddhists meditate to free their minds from the aggression, envy and greed which are a normal part of the human condition. By doing this they can allow natural calm and wisdom to come through.

When Buddhists enter the shrine room in the temple and see a statue of the Buddha they are inspired by the loving kindness, compassion, joy and serenity of the Master – states of being to which they all aspire. Meditation and prayer are two spiritual disciplines which can be used to attain them.

Prayer

Buddhists in Nepal and Tibet use prayer beads (*mala*) to help them pray. The *mala* can have 108, 54 or 27 beads which are made of seeds, wood or plastic. Buddhists use the beads to count the number of times they fall prostrate and to aid concentration. With each bead a mantra is chanted or the name of a buddha or Bodhisattva is recited. The circle of beads sometimes contains three larger beads to remind worshippers of the Three Refuges – the Buddha, the Dharma and the *Sangha*.

Tibetan Buddhists believe that when mantras are recited many times they arouse good vibrations within the person. Repeated often enough the mantra can open up the mind to a higher form of consciousness. The greatest mantra – *Om mani padme hum* – is known as the 'jewel in the lotus' since it is thought to encompass the heart of the Buddha's teaching. The 'jewel' is also inscribed on revolving brass cylinders called prayer wheels. Every temple and vihara has a set of prayer wheels which people spin so that the vibrations are sent in all directions.

Meditation

As the Buddha reached enlightenment through meditation it is important for all Buddhists – ordained and lay. There are two basic forms:

◆ *Samatha* is designed to lead to mind development and genuine mental tranquillity. Normally the mind is in a state of constant flux owing to distractions from the senses,

Turning prayer wheels. Each wheel has a chant, or mantra, written across its surface, so that the mantra is repeated many times as the wheel spins round.

Although the *mala* can include as many as 108 beads, this number makes for a noisy and clumsy meditation tool, so it is only used by priests. Lay Buddhists are more likely to use just 27 beads, including larger beads at positions 1, 7 and 21 so they can remember the Three Refuges – the Buddha, the Dharma and the *Sangha*.

Prayer does not exist in Buddhism as such because there's no one to talk to. In my devotions I say to myself, 'To the best of my ability, I shall try to emulate the life of the Buddha.' So I have my shrine room, and even my children, before they go to their work or to their colleges, do their devotion, and only after their devotion, they set out. It's almost the same as having a portrait of your parents to remind you of the love that they had for you.

FROM AN INTERVIEW WITH A BUDDHIST ON *WORLDS OF FAITH*, BBC RADIO 4, 1983

the desires and reflection. This kind of meditation frees the mind and gives it a single focus.

◆ *Vipassana* is designed to give insights into the truths of impermanence (*anicca*), suffering (*dukkha*) and 'no self' (*anatman*).

Vipassana is superior to *samatha* because it is distinctively Buddhist and produces the kind of understanding which leads to enlightenment. It forms the basis of teaching in all Theravada meditation centres.

Festivals and Celebrations

The Buddha taught that people should not attach any spiritual significance to festivals, so Buddhists do not rate them very highly. What matters is the attitude of mind in those who are celebrating.

The date and meaning of each Buddhist festival depend on the traditions and culture of each particular country. Many festivals celebrate the Buddha's life, teaching and enlightenment. Others celebrate Bodhisattvas, important teachers or events in Buddhist history. Often alongside these Buddhist festivals are national times of celebration which mark events in the agricultural year.

Wesak **day**

The birth, enlightenment and death of the Buddha are all believed to have occurred on the same day in the month of *Wesak* (May to June). Buddhists celebrate these events on *Wesak* day. They decorate their houses and make offerings in the temple. They use candles and other lights to symbolize the Buddha's enlightenment. *Wesak* day is also believed to be the time when Buddha preached

Devotion to the Buddha is part of everyday life in countries with a large Buddhist following, such as Sri Lanka and Thailand. Here, temples, shrines and monasteries are familiar sights.

the first Dharma and it is marked by a joyful festival in many Buddhist countries.

Uposatha days

Uposatha days are those which are related to the phases of the moon and other special days in the lunar calendar. *Uposatha* means 'entering to stay' and on these days lay Buddhists wear special clothes, usually white robes, and enter the local vihara to join the monks in chanting and singing. They also spend a lot of time meditating, as well as taking on the 10 precepts for the day which allow them to gain extra merit for their next reincarnation.

With this lamp which blazes with firm strength, destroying darkness, I make offering to the truly enlightened lamp of the world, the dispeller of darkness. With this fragrant smoke full of perfume I make offering to the one worthy to receive them.

A PRAYER FOR *WESAK* DAY

with relics of the Buddha, such as the well-known Festival of the Sacred Tooth at Kandy in Sri Lanka.

Many Buddhists send each other *Wesak* cards, which are decorated with a lotus, the symbol of purity, or a picture of the Buddha's birth, enlightenment or death, or perhaps a *bodhi* tree.

Local festivals

In addition to the main festivals there are others which are just celebrated locally. Some of these are associated

RAINY SEASON

During the rainy season, or *Asalha*, the Buddha is believed to have entered heaven and taught the Dharma to the gods. During this time of year, travelling in many Buddhist countries is difficult so the monks remain in their monasteries to meditate and study. At the end of *Asalha* the monks conduct a special ceremony in which they ask their fellow monks for forgiveness if they have offended them at any time. Lay Buddhists make practical gifts to the monks; this festival of giving is called *Kathina*.

Buddhism Today

During the 20th century, Buddhists suffered persecution and suppression in many parts of the world. Elsewhere, however, Buddhism continued to expand. Since the early 1970s Buddhism has gained a foothold in many Western countries, notably Britain and the USA.

For the first 1,500 years of its existence, Buddhism expanded rapidly with Burma (now Myanmar), Sri Lanka, Thailand, China, Japan and Korea all embracing the religion. It then slipped into a quiet period with little happening until the start of the 20th century. Buddhism has now revived and is starting to grow again in many places.

Buddhism in the East

During the 20th century many Buddhist countries came under Communist control and the religion was suppressed. There were over 6,000 monasteries in Tibet before the Chinese invaded in the 1950s, but since then many have been destroyed. About 100,000 Tibetan Buddhists are thought to have escaped to India, and in Tibet Buddhism is still fighting for its life. Mongolia came under Communist rule in 1924 and for over 60 years no Buddhist novices could be trained as monks.

Almost all Buddhist temples in China were closed or destroyed during the Cultural Revolution (1966–76). In 1977, though, temples were allowed to reopen

BUDDHISM IN THE WEST

In the last 30 years Buddhism has spread rapidly in Western countries, due largely to increased travel to Buddhist areas of the world. The practice of meditation in Theravada, Zen and Tibetan Buddhism has provided an attractive alternative to many people's materialism. There are also new orders springing up such as the Friends of the Western Buddhist Order, which adapts traditional Buddhist teachings to make them more appealing to Westerners. According to the Buddhist Directory there are now over 270 Buddhist groups and centres in the UK and Ireland which offer instruction in meditation and the Buddhist way of life.

Buddhism thrives in its traditional areas, having recovered from persecution in Tibet and Mongolia, and is spreading beyond Asia. A steady demand for images of the Buddha is good for business.

and from 1980 the training of monks was permitted again. Buddhism is growing in China once more, especially in the north of the country, and gaining a large following among young people attracted by its philosophy.

Elsewhere, Buddhism is thriving. In Sri Lanka Buddhism is the majority faith of the people, while in Thailand and Bhutan it is the state religion. It is making deep inroads into Indonesia, Singapore and South Korea, while India's Buddhist minority is expanding. In India in recent years several million Hindu 'untouchables' have converted to Buddhism.

Christians believe that Jesus Christ is both the Son of God and the Son of man – fully divine, fully human and without sin. Jesus was born in Palestine 2,000 years ago, travelled around preaching and healing, was crucified on the instructions of the Roman governor and returned to life shortly afterwards. Through Christ's death and rising to life, sins have been forgiven by God, making it possible to enter eternal life with him. Most Christians express their faith by sharing regularly in Communion.

Today Christianity is the largest religion in the world with an estimated 2,000 million followers altogether, although it is divided into more than 20,000 different denominations or Churches. The largest of these is the

The cross is the most evocative symbol of Christianity. Jesus Christ died on a cross 2,000 years ago, but then returned to life.

Roman Catholic Church, with 1,200 million followers, followed by the many Protestant Churches, with 360 million in total, and the Orthodox Church, with 170 million. The largest of the Protestant Churches is the Anglican Church, with 80 million members.

> *The Christian religion not only was at first attended with miracles, but even at this day cannot be believed by any reasonable person without one. Mere reason is insufficient to convince us of its veracity; and whoever is moved by faith to assent to it, is conscious of a continued miracle in his own understanding.*
>
> DAVID HUME (1711–76),
> SCOTTISH PHILOSOPHER

CHRISTIANITY

Contents

Who is Jesus?

By the time Jesus was born, around 4 BCE, the Jews had been waiting centuries for the Messiah foretold by their scriptures. Jesus, though, was reluctant to accept this title for himself because of the connotations it carried. The kingdom he came to build was spiritual, not political – one built in people's hearts.

After Jesus ascended to heaven his followers wasted no time in preaching that he was the Messiah – the one who would deliver them. This precipitated a final break between Judaism and Christianity, because the Jews rejected the claim, whereas the early Christians placed it at the heart of their preaching. They even took the Greek word for 'Messiah' – *christus*, meaning 'anointed by God' – and turned it into a surname for Jesus.

Why were they so sure Jesus was the long-awaited Messiah? The time they had spent with him had convinced them: he fed large crowds miraculously, he cast out demons, he forgave sins and he announced the coming of God's kingdom. This was just the kind of thing that the divine Messiah was expected to do.

The Son of God and the Son of man

The early Christians often called Jesus the 'Son of God', although

> *'Who do you say I am?' Simon Peter answered, 'You are the Messiah, the Son of the living God.' 'Good for you, Simon son of John!' answered Jesus. 'For this truth did not come to you from any human being, but it was given to you directly by my Father in heaven.'*
> MATTHEW 16:15–17

the phrase only crops up occasionally in the Gospels. The title highlights the unique relationship that Jesus enjoyed with God – best compared to the relationship between father and son. Jesus shocked his disciples by calling God 'Abba', a term which suggested the closest possible relationship.

For his part, however, Jesus preferred to call himself the 'Son of man'. It was a phrase familiar to his listeners since it was used many times in the Jewish scriptures. There it usually referred simply to 'humankind', but it could also denote a figure of great spiritual authority who, at the end of time, would be given an everlasting kingdom by God to rule over.

If we put these terms together, we gain some idea of how Jesus saw himself and of how others saw him. As the Messiah he came to deliver people from their sins; as God's Son he enjoyed a unique relationship with God and yet, as the Son of man, he identified himself with all human beings.

By the time of Jesus, pious Jews had awaited the coming of the Messiah – God's special messenger – for centuries. They hoped he would free them from the yoke of subservience to Rome, but few were prepared for a Messiah, who, through his death, freed all people from their slavery to sin. *Christ en Croix (Christ on the Cross)* by Georges Roualt (1871–1958).

The Ministry of Jesus

Although Jesus was not actually a rabbi his followers regarded him as one – and one who taught with much greater authority than the contemporary Jewish teachers. The miracles Jesus performed were a central part of his ministry, showing the people that God himself was working among them.

A t the beginning of his ministry Jesus taught in the Jewish synagogues, as any Jewish male was entitled to do. When this proved no longer possible because of the

Jesus' miracles caught people's attention and demonstrated that God was intervening supernaturally in his world. *Jesus Opens the Eyes of a Man Born Blind* by Duccio di Buoninsegna (c. 1255–c. 1318).

strength of opposition to him, he taught his disciples, and the people, in the open air or in the houses of his friends. The people brought their questions about the Jewish law to him, and he taught them about such things as paying taxes to the Romans, adultery, marriage and divorce, love and forgiveness. By seeking his guidance on the law the people were treating him like a rabbi.

Jesus often responded to them with parables – stories drawn from everyday life which carry a spiritual meaning. The

> *The time has arrived; the kingdom of God is upon you. Repent, and believe the gospel.*
>
> MARK 1:15

Jewish holy books were full of such stories. Nearly all Jesus' parables were designed to let people know he had brought God's kingdom and to show how they could enter it.

Jesus' miracles

In a sermon he preached in the synagogue in Nazareth Jesus told his listeners what the prophet Isaiah had said about the Messiah: he would 'bring good news to the poor... liberty to the captives and recovery of sight to the blind'. The most striking feature of Jesus' ministry in all four Gospels is the miracles he performed. We frequently see a Jesus who had the power to cure disease, cast out evil spirits, feed the hungry, tame the unruly elements of nature and bring the dead back to life. The Gospels show Jesus was often moved by people's needs and that he responded to their faith in him.

The Gospels of Matthew, Mark and Luke contain about 40 different parables of Jesus; one of the best known is 'The Good Samaritan'. John's Gospel has no parables, but includes Jesus' 'I am' sayings, for example, 'I am the bread of life'.

WORD OF MOUTH

The only real information we have about Jesus comes from the four Gospels in the New Testament of the Bible. The first of these, Mark, was not written until some 35 years after his death. During the intervening period memories of his actions and teachings were passed on by word of mouth. Oral tradition also held an important place in Jewish history and the teachings of all prophets and leaders were kept alive in this way for centuries.

Death and Resurrection

The death and resurrection of Jesus form the bedrock of the Christian faith. Through Christ's death Christians believe that their sins have been forgiven while his resurrection assures them that death is not the end.

The Gospels of Matthew, Mark and Luke make it clear that opposition to Jesus and his teaching began almost at the same time as his public ministry. The Roman rulers suspected him of inciting the people to rebellion, while the religious leaders considered his actions blasphemous and believed he was encouraging people to break the Jewish law. Many ordinary people, though, supported him almost to the end.

The death of Jesus

On the night before his death, Jesus met with his disciples in Jerusalem to celebrate the Jewish Passover. During the meal, Jesus used the bread and wine to teach his disciples about the meaning of his impending death. This meal – the Last Supper – has been commemorated by Christians ever since through the regular celebration of Communion.

After the meal, Jesus went out of the city and spent some time praying to God. Soon afterwards, he was arrested and taken before the High Priest, the Jewish Council (the Sanhedrin) and Pontius Pilate, the Roman governor. Pilate alone could pass the death sentence and, after intense pressure from the crowds, that's just what he did.

Jesus was crucified – nailed to a cross until he died of asphyxiation – just outside Jerusalem, an event which Christians throughout the world remember on Good Friday. A secret follower of Jesus, Joseph of Arimathea, asked Pilate for Jesus' dead body, which he laid in his own unused tomb.

The Gospels record seven 'last words' from Jesus on the cross. These utterances have long played a central role in Christian devotions during Good Friday.

> For us and for our salvation [he] came down from heaven; by the power of the Holy Spirit he became incarnate of the Virgin Mary and was made man. For our sake he was crucified under Pontius Pilate; he suffered death and was buried. On the third day he rose again in accordance with the scriptures.
>
> NICENE CREED

allowed. When the women arrived at the tomb they found the stone rolled away from its entrance and the tomb empty. They met an angel who told them that Jesus had been brought back to life. On the same day, Jesus himself appeared among the disciples, then twice more after that. In the weeks that followed the news that Jesus was alive was broadcast to more and more people.

The truth about Jesus' resurrection dawned very slowly on his disciples. Gradually they came to understand that Jesus was a new kind of Messiah – not an earthly king but a heavenly ruler. Forty days later the disciples were present when Jesus disappeared from their sight into heaven, an event which some Christians celebrate on Ascension Day. Before he left earth, Jesus promised his disciples he would send them a comforter or helper – his Holy Spirit – who would always be with them.

Crucifixion was a cruel means of execution. But Jesus' resurrection turned an apparently terrible defeat into a glorious victory over sin and death. This sculpture is in a church in Bristol, England.

The resurrection of Jesus

Three days later three women visited the tomb to embalm Jesus' body. This task was normally carried out immediately after death but Jesus had died too close to the start of the Jewish Sabbath day, during which no work was

The Early Church

Luke ends his Gospel with Jesus promising his Holy Spirit to his disciples before departing from them. He begins his second book, the Acts of the Apostles, with the same promise, followed by Jesus' ascension into heaven. He then goes on to describe the birth of the Christian Church during the Jewish feast of Pentecost.

Jews came from all over the Roman empire to Jerusalem for Pentecost, a festival which celebrated when God gave the Torah to Moses on Mount Sinai.

The Day of Pentecost

For the previous few weeks the disciples had huddled together in Jerusalem hoping they would not meet the same fate as Jesus. During this time they recalled Jesus' promise that they would receive God's power when the Holy Spirit came and that they would carry his message throughout Jerusalem, Judea, Samaria and beyond. Luke gives two pieces of descriptive information in his account:

◆ The disciples heard a sound, like a mighty rushing wind, coming from heaven.
◆ The disciples saw what appeared to be flames of fire resting on each of them.

Thus the Christian Church was born on the Day of Pentecost.

> *Peter replied, 'Repent and be baptized, every one of you, in the name of Jesus Christ so that your sins may be forgiven. And you will receive the gift of the Holy Spirit. The promise is for you and your children and for all who are far off — for all whom the Lord our God will call.'*
>
> ACTS 2:38–39

♦ Jesus was the Messiah.
♦ The Messiah had been crucified and brought back to life.
♦ Jesus had now been given the highest place in heaven by God.
♦ All those who repent of their sins and believe in Jesus are forgiven by God.

These four beliefs became the heart of the Church's preaching and message.

Christians throughout the world celebrate this each year at the festival of Pentecost.

Peter's sermon

Throughout Jesus' ministry, and during the days following his death, Peter had been the main spokesman for the disciples. After the disciples received the Holy Spirit, Peter delivered a sermon to the people of Jerusalem in which he made four important points about Jesus:

As Peter preached, following the outpouring of the Holy Spirit on the Day of Pentecost, 3,000 people responded and the Christian Church was born. Peter, portrayed in stained glass, holding the keys to heaven and hell.

> *I am convinced that neither death nor life, neither angels nor demons, neither the present nor the future, nor any powers, neither height nor depth, nor anything else in all creation, will be able to separate us from the love of God that is in Christ Jesus our Lord.*
>
> ROMANS 8:38–39

Tough times ahead

The commitment of the early Church to welcoming Jews and Gentiles alike was largely the work of the apostle Paul. Between 45 and 62 CE he carried the Christian message into Asia Minor, Greece and finally to Rome. He taught that everyone could find salvation as long as they believed the gospel – the 'good news' – because of the death and resurrection of Jesus. Paul also wrote many letters to teach and encourage the churches he had founded. These were circulated and greatly treasured.

One Church – Many Churches

Until the downfall of the Roman empire the Church was undivided – if not always united. With the loss of its Roman power base in the West, however, power within the Church shifted to the East.

A council of bishops meeting at Chalcedon in 451 CE adopted a resolution that many from the East could not accept. As a result the Church began to show the first signs of disintegration with the formation of the Eastern Orthodox Church. It was not until 1054, however, that the split between East and West became final with the Orthodox Church severing all links with the Roman Catholic Church. There were three main areas of disagreement:

◆ The claim of the Pope in Rome to have supreme authority over the whole Church.
◆ The desire of Rome to be the acknowledged leader of the worldwide Church.
◆ A change by Rome to the wording of the Creed, considered to be inviolable by Eastern Christians.

The Reformation

In the centuries that followed, dissatisfaction built up within the Roman Catholic Church. Matters came to a head in 1517 when Martin Luther, a German monk, nailed a list of 95 theses (grievances) against the Catholic Church to the door of his own church in Wittenburg, Germany. Luther argued the authority of the Bible was far more important than that of the Pope or the Church, and that salvation could come only by faith and not by good works as the Church was teaching. His protest led to the beginning of the Reformation and the birth of the Protestant Church.

The Reformation aimed at reforming the abuses in the Roman Catholic Church and ended in schism. Its chief leaders were Ulrich Zwingli and John Calvin in Switzerland and Martin Luther in Germany. Before long the Reformation had spread to Holland, France, Hungary, England and Scotland and it reached the USA in the 17th century.

The Christian Church today is unbelievably fragmented. There are thought to be over 22,500 recognized Churches and denominations in existence.

Reformed Churches

Before long the Church of England began to splinter and the Reformed Churches (those which did not accept the teachings of the Church of England) came into existence. The Baptist Church, with its core belief that adult Christians rather than children should be baptized, was formed in the early 17th century. The Quakers, convinced that nonviolence is the only true Christian path, were formed in the 1650s. The Methodist Church, which was largely based on the teachings of the Anglican clergyman John Wesley, was formed at the end of the 18th century. At the end of the 19th century the Salvation Army had a great impact with activities directed at the poor, the outcast and the destitute. Today the Salvation Army works in 94 countries and its influence is felt worldwide. Before very long all of these Churches were to spread to many other countries. The Baptist and Methodist Churches, for instance, were to become very influential in the USA and they remain so today.

The Bible

The Bible is the holy book for Christians and widely used in both private and public worship. Many believe it to be divinely inspired. The writing within the Bible ranges from history, law and prophecy to poetry and wisdom, letters and Gospels.

The Bible is a collection of books divided into two parts – the Old Testament and the New Testament.

The Old Testament

The Jewish scriptures have 24 books but many were divided to form the 39 books of the Christian Old Testament. To this foundation were added the 27 books of the New Testament, a collection of books of Christian origin. The earliest

Christians had the Jewish scriptures as their Bible and when the apostle Paul wrote, 'All scripture is inspired by God,' this is what he was referring to.

Jews placed the greatest emphasis on the first five books of the Old Testament, the Torah, but Christians were interested in themes that ran throughout the whole of the Old Testament. These were, they believed, fulfilled in Jesus and in the early Church, the new Israel, which

The Bible, either wholly or partly, has been translated into 2,261 languages. The whole Bible is available in 383 languages. The Bible is used in every kind of setting, from the liturgy of the cathedral to individual or group study in homes.

was continuing his work. They were particularly concerned to show that what they believed about Jesus, the Messiah, was firmly rooted in the Old Testament. The phrase 'so that the scripture might be fulfilled' is used frequently in Matthew's Gospel.

The New Testament

The New Testament contains 27 books in all – four Gospels, the Acts of the Apostles, 21 letters or epistles (13 of which carry the name of Paul) and the book of Revelation. Most of these books

Beautifully inscribed and illustrated Bibles were treasured in Europe in the Middle Ages. A copy could be as valuable as a small farm.

But for your part, stand by the truths you have learned and are assured of. Remember from whom you learned them; remember that from early childhood you have been familiar with the sacred writings which have power to make you wise and lead you to salvation through faith in Christ Jesus.

All inspired scripture has its use for teaching the truth and refuting error, or for reformation of manners and discipline in right living.

2 TIMOTHY 3:14–16

were written within a generation or two of Jesus' death.

◆ Of the four Gospels three present a similar picture of Jesus and have much of their material in common. They are called the synoptic Gospels – Matthew, Mark and Luke – and were probably written between 65 and 80 CE. The fourth, John, was written some time later.

◆ The Acts of the Apostles, by Gospel-writer Luke, is a record of the early Church from Jesus' ascension into heaven to around the end of Paul's life.

◆ We do not know how many of the New Testament epistles were actually written by Paul since many which traditionally carry his name did not come from his pen. John and Peter also wrote letters included in the New Testament as did other early Church leaders.

◆ The book of Revelation records John's vision of Jesus' authority over heaven and earth, given to him by God. It is quite unlike any other book in the New Testament.

Beliefs

Beliefs determine the way men and women approach God and conduct their spiritual life.

Creeds are Christian statements of belief. Christians have composed several of them in the last 2,000 years, although only two – the Apostles' Creed and the Nicene Creed – have been widely used in worship. Both these Creeds were formulated in the early centuries of Christian faith and Roman Catholic, Orthodox and Anglican Churches still use them in some services.

Tenets of faith
Over the centuries several salient aspects of Christian belief have emerged:

◆ The Trinity is God as three persons in one – God the Father, God the Son and God the Holy Spirit. Belief in the Trinity underpins the Christian faith and is implicit in both the Apostles' and Nicene Creeds.
◆ The incarnation refers to the birth of God in human flesh in the form of Jesus and emphasizes that Jesus was fully God and yet fully human.
◆ The atonement is the reconciliation between God and people achieved by Jesus' death and resurrection. Jesus is the supreme example to the world of self-sacrifice – the ultimate offering to God so that the sins of the world can be forgiven. Everything accomplished by the death of Jesus is sealed by his resurrection from the dead.
◆ The Holy Spirit is a member of the Trinity and God's power in the world today. Many Christians believe the Holy Spirit inspired the writing of the scriptures and still speaks through them today. He helps people to pray and inspires

> *I believe in God, the Father Almighty, creator of heaven and earth. I believe in Jesus Christ, his only Son, our Lord. He was conceived by the power of the Holy Spirit and born of the Virgin Mary. He suffered under Pontius Pilate, was crucified, died and was buried... On the third day he rose again. He ascended into heaven and is seated on the right hand of the Father. He will come again to judge the living and the dead.*
> *I believe in the Holy Spirit; the holy, catholic Church, the communion of saints, the forgiveness of sins, the resurrection of the body and the life everlasting. Amen.*
> APOSTLES' CREED

Christian thinkers have tried to find analogies for the Trinity drawn from everyday experience. One suggestion is water, which retains its chemical identity even when it takes the form of ice, liquid or steam.

those seeking to build God's kingdom on earth.

◆ Many Christians hold that the Bible is divinely inspired and without error, authoritative in all matters of belief and behaviour. For others, the Bible is less a blueprint, more a guide laying down principles for everyday Christian living.

◆ For Catholic and Orthodox Christians the Virgin Mary has a status far above simply being the mother of Jesus.

They believe she conceived Jesus supernaturally through the Holy Spirit, retained her virginity to the end of her life, was taken up bodily into heaven without experiencing death, and is now so close to God that she is able to represent the needs of all those still on earth. Protestants believe that Mary was God's chosen vehicle to give birth to Jesus – but no more.

Central to all the Creeds is the death of Jesus as a sacrifice for human sin. *Crucifixion* from a French Book of Hours, Paris, 1407.

Sacraments

Sacraments stand at the heart of worship in Roman Catholic and Orthodox Churches, as they do for many Christians from the Anglican and Episcopalian traditions. However, they have a much lower profile in Reformed Churches.

The sacraments are ceremonies or rituals which can be traced back to Jesus' ministry or the worship of the early Christians. They make tangible the mystery of Christ's incarnation, death and resurrection for worshippers, using a material element – such as bread, wine, water or oil – to convey a spiritual blessing.

Communion is the 'meal' of bread and wine at which Christians remember and share in the death of Jesus on the cross. There are various names for the services in which Communion takes place: Roman Catholics call it the Mass, Orthodox Christians the Divine Liturgy, Baptists the Lord's Supper, and Anglicans the Eucharist.

Roman Catholic and Orthodox sacraments

Roman Catholic and Orthodox worshippers celebrate seven sacraments, or 'mysteries', as the Orthodox Church prefers to call them:

> *Q: What meanest thou by this word sacrament?*
> *A: I mean an outward and visible sign of an inward and spiritual grace.*
> ANGLICAN *BOOK OF COMMON PRAYER*

The bread and wine, symbols of the death of Jesus, used in Communion.

◆ Penance is the confession of and forgiveness (absolution) for sin.

◆ Extreme unction is the anointing of the sick with oil. In the Roman Catholic Church the last rites are administered to dying people and this includes the viaticum – their last taking of Communion.

◆ Holy orders describes the status of deacons, priests or bishops, who are able to serve the church and administer the sacraments.

◆ Matrimony in the Roman Catholic tradition involves taking Communion (the nuptial Mass) in which, exceptionally, the man and woman give the elements of bread and wine to each other.

Christian marriage is seen as a threefold partnership involving husband, wife and God.

◆ Communion, the meal of bread and wine, which is part of the Mass in Roman Catholic Churches and part of the Divine Liturgy in Orthodox Churches.

◆ Baptism is the initiation ceremony into Church membership and symbolizes the cleansing of a person from sin. Most Churches baptize infants, although the Baptists, and some others, only baptize believing adults.

◆ Confirmation is entering into full Church membership.

Most Protestant Churches recognize and celebrate the sacraments of Communion and Baptism – although the Quakers and the Salvation Army do not celebrate any sacraments. Many also have services of confirmation, matrimony and ordination but they do not consider them to be sacraments.

Church Buildings

Over the centuries some Christians have used the size and craftsmanship of their places of worship to express their belief in the greatness of God. Others, though, have deliberately kept their churches and chapels plain and small to show that simplicity should be the key to true worship.

Different Christian Churches worship God in their own ways and this is reflected in their places of worship. There are, however, features which most churches have in common.

The altar

Altars are found in Orthodox, Roman Catholic and Anglican churches. In older churches, when the worshipper faces the altar, he or she is also facing eastwards to the holy city of Jerusalem, but in more modern churches, the altar is often placed in the middle of the church with the congregation gathered around it.

The altar represents the table at which Jesus shared the Last Supper with his disciples. It is the place from which the

The altar is the focal point of worship in Orthodox, Roman Catholic and many Anglican Churches.

bread and wine are dispensed during Communion.

The pulpit

Pulpits are raised platforms from which sermons are preached and are the focal point in Baptist, Lutheran, Methodist and Pentecostal churches. This shows their emphasis on the preaching of the Bible rather than on the celebration of the sacraments.

Stained-glass windows

Windows composed of sections of stained glass depicting biblical themes are found in many older churches. In the past, they were used as visual aids to teach the largely illiterate congregations stories from the Bible.

The font

Fonts hold the water used for baptism and are found in churches offering the sacrament of infant baptism. In most churches the font is located just inside the door to show that baptism is the 'door' through which a child passes into church membership. In some churches, however, the font is portable and is placed in the middle of the

In 1989 there were 38,607 Churches of all denominations in England. By 1998 the figure was 37,717. During this period 1,867 new buildings were opened and 2,667 closed leading to a net loss in the period of 800 Churches.

congregation for the service, showing how baptism brings a baby into the 'family' of the church.

The confessional

In older Catholic churches the confessional is a wooden cubicle with a grill down the middle to separate the priest from the penitent – the person making the confession. Since the

The font, where babies are christened, is located near the door of a church, as a reminder that baptism is the means of entry into God's family.

Second Vatican Council of the Roman Catholic Church (1962–65), however, priest and penitent have been encouraged to talk face to face when participating in the Sacrament of Reconciliation, as confession is now called.

In many places the church is not simply a place of worship but also a centre to be used for the benefit of the whole community. Different denominations often unite and use the building for joint activities.

Communion

Based upon the last meal that Jesus shared with his disciples, Communion is first mentioned in one of Paul's letters. It has always been the central act of worship for most Christians.

The Jewish festival of Passover celebrates the time when God saved the Israelites from Egyptian slavery and made a covenant with them. Christians believe that, with the death and resurrection of Jesus, a new covenant was made between God and his 'new Israel' – the Church. Jesus was a perfect sacrifice, offered once and for all for the sins of the world, and this is celebrated during Communion.

It was during his Last Supper with his disciples that Jesus spoke of the bread as his body, broken for humanity, and the wine as his blood, poured out for us.

Celebrating Communion

Roman Catholics call their Communion service 'Mass', from the concluding words of the old Latin service, *Ite, missa est* – 'Go, you are sent on a mission.' The daily celebration of Mass includes the confession of sins; the Liturgy of the Word, which includes three readings from the Bible, a sermon, or homily,

and the Nicene Creed; and the Liturgy of the Eucharist. In the Liturgy of the Eucharist the priest consecrates the bread, or host, and wine, raises the host to God and offers it to each worshipper. In some countries the people are offered the host alone, while in others the priest gives them both the bread and wine.

TRANSUBSTANTIATION

Broadly speaking, there are two very different ways of understanding Communion.

Roman Catholics believe the bread and wine become the actual body and blood of Jesus after they have been consecrated. This is known as transubstantiation. This belief is held by many Anglican and Orthodox Christians as well.

Reformed Christians take the bread and wine to be just symbols which help them to remember, and be thankful for, the death of Jesus for their sins.

Communion is at the heart of worship for most Christians. Here a communicant receives the wine.

There is a close similarity between the words used in the Catholic Mass and in Protestant Communion services, where the sacrament is usually offered once each Sunday and at least once during the week.

In Reformed Churches, however, the Lord's Supper is offered twice a month and on special days such as Maundy Thursday. Here the service is conducted by the minister, who stands behind the Communion table along with the lay leaders of the congregation. The bread is in small pieces and the wine is in tiny glasses and these are taken to members of the congregation where they are sitting. The people usually eat the bread upon receiving it, to symbolize their personal

The Lord Jesus, on the night he was betrayed, took a piece of bread, gave thanks to God, broke it, and said, 'This is my body, which is for you. Do this in memory of me.' In the same way, after supper he took the cup and said, 'This cup is God's new covenant, sealed with my blood. Whenever you drink it, do so in memory of me.'

1 CORINTHIANS 11:23–25

response to Christ, but they drink the wine together to show their spiritual unity.

Baptism

The sacrament of baptism is one of the earliest Christian rituals. Baptism of adults by full immersion was the rite of admission to the Christian community until the fourth century, when high infant mortality led to demands by Christian parents for their babies to be baptized.

Infant baptism is now the norm in Roman Catholic, Orthodox and most Protestant Churches, although other denominations, such as the Baptists, only carry out the baptism of believing adults.

Infant baptism

Roman Catholic and Anglican infant baptism services share significant features. The ceremony, conducted by a priest, is held around the font where the child is presented for baptism by parents and godparents. They promise to teach the child to fight against evil, to instruct the child in the teachings of Jesus Christ, and to bring the child up in the family of God, the Church. The priest sprinkles the baby with water three times in the name of the Father, the Son and the Holy Spirit, before making the sign of the cross on its forehead.

In the Orthodox Church, the priest blesses and breathes on the water before anointing the baby with the 'oil of gladness'. The naked baby is placed in the font, facing east, and immersed in the water three times. The service of chrismation is carried out directly afterwards, with the

A baby is baptized in an Anglican Church. After sprinkling the child with water, the priest makes the sign of the cross on his or her forehead. The parents decide to have their baby baptized on his or her behalf.

They argue that the Church is a fellowship of believers who accept that Jesus died for them and, having been raised from the dead, now lives in them through his Holy Spirit. They confess this belief before they are baptized. The Baptist Church in particular emphasizes that all examples of baptism in the New Testament involved believing adults.

Baptism in itself does not accomplish anything. It is simply an outward and highly symbolic act indicating a series of spiritual changes within the believer. There are three pieces of symbolism in believer's baptism:

◆ As the person goes down into the water they show that they are dying with Christ to sin.
◆ The brief time beneath the water indicates that they are 'buried with Christ'.
◆ Leaving the pool shows the person has 'risen with Christ' and is starting a new spiritual life.

Believer's baptism is offered by many Churches to adults who have come to their own faith in Christ. Going down into the water and up out of it again symbolizes the person dying to themselves and then being resurrected as a new person in Christ.

baby dressed in new clothes. This is equivalent to confirmation in many other Churches.

Believer's baptism

Many Christians believe that infant baptism is inappropriate.

Then Jesus came from Galilee to the Jordan to be baptized by John. But John tried to deter him, saying, 'I need to be baptized by you, and do you come to me?' Jesus replied, 'Let it be so now; it is proper for us to do this to fulfil all righteousness.' Then John consented. As soon as Jesus was baptized, he went up out of the water.

MATTHEW 3:13–16

Death and Eternal Life

The Christian Church has always held clearly defined views about life after death. Underlying each funeral service is the belief that death is not the end, but the gateway to eternal life.

Beliefs about what happens after death are reflected in the funeral services held by the different denominations.

Roman Catholic funerals

Catholic funerals traditionally include prayers in the dead person's house with an all-night vigil around the coffin. Nowadays, however, the coffin is usually left overnight in church, where the mourners gather to pray for the dead person's soul. The priest dresses in white for the service,

> *I am the resurrection and the life. Those who believe in me will live, even though they die; and all those who live and believe in me will never die.*
>
> JOHN 11:25–26

the colour associated with death and life after death. These twin themes form the basis of the funeral.

The priest meets the coffin at the door of the church, sprinkles it with holy water and recites words from

Although the passing away of a friend or relative is a sad occasion, for Christians it is the means of entry into a new and endless relationship with Christ, free from all sin and suffering. An open coffin in a Samoan funeral service.

John's Gospel. In the prayers which follow the hope is expressed that the dead person will be eternally happy and will rise up to meet Christ on the Day of Judgment. Roman Catholics believe that, after death, a person's soul waits in purgatory, where it is cleansed before entering heaven – so they pray for it, hoping to shorten the length of time it spends there.

Protestant funerals

When a person has died their soul is committed to God's safe keeping in a short service comprising hymns, prayers, Bible readings and a eulogy. Everything in the service underlines the Protestant belief that once a Christian dies their soul goes straight to God in heaven. It also looks forward to the time when the dead will be raised up and Christ's kingdom will be established on earth.

> *Rejoice for a brother deceased; our loss is his infinite gain.*
>
> CHARLES WESLEY (1707–88), ENGLISH HYMNWRITER

Orthodox funerals

A fundamental belief of Orthodox Christianity is that there is no difference between the living and the dead – everyone is part of the eternal and worldwide Church. Just as we pray for those who are alive so we must pray for those who have died. The Orthodox Church tries to take the mystery and fear out of death.

As soon as someone has died their body is washed, dressed in new clothes and placed in an open coffin. A strip of material containing icons of John the Baptist, the Virgin Mary and Jesus is placed across the corpse's forehead and an icon put in the hand. The body is then covered with a linen cloth to symbolize the protection that Christ offers to all, alive and dead. The coffin lid is only closed for the last time when the service is finished.

Everything in the Orthodox service is a reminder that death is a direct result of the sin that separates God and the human race. Yet even in such sadness there is real hope, symbolized by the burning candles and incense which are a central part of the service. The Bible readings encourage everyone to look forward to the time when Christ will return to earth and all will be raised from death.

Worship and Prayer

Worship attempts to bridge the inevitable gap between God and the worshipper. It is offered in the knowledge that God is beyond human understanding and that any language about him is inadequate. Prayer forms a key part of all Christian services, yet private prayer is just as important. God is a personal God and in private Christians can communicate more closely with him.

There are two broad patterns of worship found in Christian Churches:

Many Churches have groups which meet to pray informally.

◆ The liturgical style depends heavily on a set pattern of worship, or liturgy, which has been hallowed through use over

a long time period. The essential elements of worship in the Eastern Orthodox Church, for instance, go back to the fourth century.

◆ The non-liturgical style is the approach used by most Protestant Churches. Here freedom of worship is emphasized – in hymn-singing, extemporaneous prayers, Bible readings and a sermon.

Prayer

The Lord's Prayer is the only prayer common to Christians of all denominations and traditions. Jesus taught it to his disciples when they asked him how they should pray. Most Christian prayers follow this example, and include praise to God, repentance for sins and seeking God's forgiveness, a request for God to intervene on behalf of the person praying and for others in need, and thankfulness to God for blessings received. Praying for others, an essential part of Christian prayer, is known as intercession.

Unlike many other religions Christianity does not lay down set times for prayer, although those following a monastic discipline do have a set routine. Many ordinary Christians make a habit of starting each day with prayer and Bible reading as well as thanking God for his loving care at the end of the day.

> *Lord Jesus Christ,*
> *Son of God, have*
> *mercy on me,*
> *a sinner.*
> THE JESUS PRAYER

THE HAIL MARY AND THE JESUS PRAYER

The Hail Mary is a prayer of praise to the Virgin Mary. It is used by Roman Catholic and Orthodox Christians, albeit in slightly different forms. Prayers to the Virgin Mary are offered in Roman Catholic and some Anglican Churches because many Christians believe she was taken directly into heaven at the end of her life, without dying. From her present exalted position close to God she is able to 'intercede' with him on behalf of those who need her help.

The Jesus Prayer, much used in the Orthodox Church, depends on repetition of Jesus' name. The common form of the prayer dates back to the sixth century. It expresses praise, as well as confidence that Jesus, the Son of God, will deliver the worshipper from all forms of sin.

Festivals

Christmas, Easter and Pentecost are the highlights of the Christian year.

Many Churches follow the Christian year closely and base their liturgy on three cycles: the Christmas, Easter and Pentecost cycles.

Advent and Christmas

The Christian year starts with Advent, on the fourth Sunday before Christmas. This season of spiritual anticipation celebrates the coming of Jesus into the world – as well as the coming of John the Baptist to prepare people for Jesus' arrival, and the Second Coming of Jesus at the end of time. Some people light Advent candles or use Advent calendars to count down the days remaining before Christmas Day – 25 December in the West.

At Christmas, Christians rejoice over the incarnation – the birth of Jesus, God's Son, as a human being – which they see as God's greatest gift to humankind.

It is traditional for churches to be lavishly decorated at this time, often incorporating a crib, and for people to exchange presents and to feast.

Lent and Holy Week

Lent is a 40-day season of repentance leading up to Easter, representing Jesus' time of temptation in the wilderness. It begins with Ash Wednesday and ends with Holy Week.

Holy Week starts with Palm Sunday, when Christians remember Jesus' triumphal entry into the city of Jerusalem on a donkey. Some believers take part in a procession to re-enact the event.

Maundy Thursday, four days later, commemorates Jesus' commandment to love one another, as well as his humility, shown through washing his disciples' feet, and the Last Supper.

For Orthodox Christians Advent is a 40-day season of penitence. Some Orthodox Churches (most notably in Russia, Georgia and Serbia) celebrate Christmas Day on 6 January, the old date for the festival.

EPIPHANY

'Epiphany' means 'manifestation' and it is a feast which takes place 12 days after Christmas. In the Eastern Church Epiphany celebrates Jesus' baptism. In the West it commemorates the visit of the Wise Men from Persia to the infant Jesus, and symbolizes Jesus' manifestation to the world.

> *They came to a place called Golgotha (which means the Place of the Skull). There they offered him wine to drink, mixed with gall; but after tasting it, he refused to drink it. When they had crucified him, they divided up his clothes by casting lots.*
>
> MATTHEW 27:33–35

The next day, Good Friday, is the most solemn in the Christian year as it marks Jesus' death. Many churches cover or remove pictures, statues and wall-hangings as a sign of respect. Different denominations may unite in a march of witness, while others take part in a vigil from noon to three o'clock to mark the last three hours of Jesus on the cross.

Easter Sunday

Easter Sunday celebrates Jesus' resurrection to new life. At midnight Orthodox worshippers pass candles from one to another, the light gradually flooding the building. Similar Saturday-evening services are held in Catholic and some Anglican Churches and end with Communion. Other Churches hold sunrise services.

Pentecost

Forty days after Easter Christians celebrate Pentecost – sometimes called Whitsun – which recalls the giving of the Holy Spirit to the first Christians in Jerusalem on the Day of Pentecost. The charismatic movement and the burgeoning Pentecostal Church are reminders that the Holy Spirit is very much a part of Christians' lives today.

The Easter services of the Orthodox Churches are steeped in ritual and tradition. A bishop blesses the crowd during an Easter celebration at Tobolsk, Siberia.

The Monastic Life

Ever since the fourth century some Christians have wanted to dedicate themselves solely to a life of austerity and prayer. The monastic movement has had a considerable influence on the Christian Church.

Shortly after the birth of the Christian Church, many people wanted to dedicate themselves totally to God and so the monastic movement was born. Like Jesus before them they took themselves off into the desert to pray. St Antony of Egypt (251–356 CE) was one of the first but he was soon followed by many others. To begin with these people lived as hermits – Antony himself spent 20 years in complete solitude – but they soon formed themselves into monastic communities. A large number of monks was drawn to Mount Athos, in northern Greece, and there are still about 20 monasteries in this area.

> *Go, sell everything you have and give to the poor, and you will have treasure in heaven. Then come, follow me.*
>
> MARK 10:21

The monks of a Greek Orthodox monastery on Mount Athos celebrate Easter.

The monastic tradition provides those who commit themselves to it with the opportunity to detach themselves from some of the stresses and distractions of life outside the monastery and so concentrate on building their relationship with God.

Religious communities

St Benedict (c. 480–c. 550) is regarded as the father of Western monasticism because he laid down the Rule by which many monasteries and convents still govern their communal life today. The Rule stipulates that each monk and nun must accept:

◆ a life of poverty. Possessions brought into the community by monks and nuns when they enter it are to be used for the benefit of all.
◆ a life of chastity. Members of a religious community must not enter into any kind of sexual or strongly emotional relationship. The Roman Catholic Church is the only Church which also demands that its priests are celibate.
◆ a life of obedience. Those who enter a religious order are expected to live in total

The monastic orders were celibate from the beginning. Celibacy did not become the norm for clergy in the Catholic Church, however, until the 12th century. By contrast, the Orthodox pattern that bishops must stay unmarried while ordinary priests can marry goes back to the earliest days of the Church.

APOSTOLIC AND CONTEMPLATIVE ORDERS

Most religious orders are 'apostolic', which means that, although their way of life involves a withdrawal from the world, they still work outside in the community – in nursing, teaching and social work, for instance.

Other religious orders are 'contemplative' with little, if any, contact with the outside world. Much stress is placed on silence within the community with contemplatives spending much of their time praying, reading holy literature and studying.

obedience to the will of the community – and ultimately of God. That will is interpreted and expressed by the leader of the community – the abbot or mother superior.

Ever since the first monasteries and convents were established their main purpose has been communal prayer. Traditionally such prayer was held seven times a day but in modern communities this has often been reduced.

Christianity Today

The Christian Church has been divided for centuries with the Eastern and Western branches operating largely independently of each other. In some parts of the world the Church is expanding rapidly while in others it is static – or in decline.

Of all today's world religions Christianity has the most members and the widest geographical spread, yet it is divided into far more branches and denominations than any other. Despite half-hearted attempts in the 20th century to bring the major Churches closer together, they are still broadly split into the Eastern and Western divisions of old. The many faces of Orthodox Christianity predominate in the Near East and Eastern Europe while Catholicism and Protestantism are in the ascendancy elsewhere.

The worldwide Church

The Christian Church world-wide takes many forms as the following illustrate:

◆ Church attendance in the USA tops 40 per cent. About 25 per cent of the American population is Catholic, with half of these attending church several times a month. The number of Catholic priests,

however, is declining rapidly – a drop of some 50 per cent between 1966 and 2000 – due largely to the priestly requirement of celibacy. The most remarkable recent growth in North America has been in Evangelical Protestant groups.

◆ Christians are now more numerous on the continent of Africa than Muslims. In recent years many charismatic Episcopalian Churches have been established and are thriving. Numerous independent Churches draw in converts but their theology is not always that of mainline Christianity.

◆ Although South Korea is traditionally a Buddhist and

In the modern world nine people convert to Islam for every three converted to Christianity.

In many parts of the world, the Christian faith is growing with phenomenal speed. In Africa it is reckoned that the rate at which the population is converting to Christianity exceeds the birth rate.

The 20th century saw more people worldwide convert to Christianity than in all the previous centuries added together.

Confucianist country the Christian Church is growing there by 10 per cent year on year. This growth is not down to the work of Christian missionaries but is a genuine grass-roots movement among the people.

◆ Liberation Theology, one of the Church's most controversial movements in the 20th century, sees Christianity as a revolutionary movement growing out of the needs of the people and their study of Jesus' teachings. The proper role of the Church, it is believed, is a political identification with the poor. Liberation Theology has been the work of Roman Catholic and, to a lesser extent, Protestant clergy in South America — as well as in Africa and Asia. Also, in South America, some forms of Evangelical Christianity have made great strides. In the early 1990s, for instance, five Evangelical Churches a week were being set up in Rio de Janeiro alone.

Islam is one of the world's newest great religions. It began in the sixth century in the area now called Saudi Arabia. Its two holiest sites, Makkah (Mecca) and Madinah (Medina), are both located here. Although Islam is a worldwide religion, the majority of its 1,200 million followers are still found in North Africa, the Middle East and South-East Asia.

Islam is an Arabic word meaning 'to submit' and a Muslim is 'one who submits to the will of Allah'. Islam is a total way of life covering both the secular and the spiritual areas of life. It is believed that from time to time Allah sent prophets such as Abraham, Moses and Jesus to show people how they should live but their message was largely ignored. Finally Allah sent

Each year around two million Muslims make a pilgrimage to Makkah, known as the Hajj.

Muhammad, the last and greatest in the prophetic line, and revealed his will to him in a series of revelations which were recorded, without error, in the Qur'an. Muslims have the greatest respect for Muhammad but he was not divine so must not be worshipped. Worship belongs to Allah alone since he is the creator and ruler of the universe.

The true believers are those who only believe in God and his messenger and afterwards doubt not, but strive with their wealth and their lives for the cause of God. Such are the sincere.

QUR'AN, 49.15

ISLAM

Contents

Muhammad's Early Years

As a young orphan Muhammad knew both poverty and sadness and this prepared him to receive his revelations from Allah. These revelations form the basis of Islam.

Muhammad was born in the city of Makkah in about 570 CE. Makkah was at the centre of a prosperous caravan route which facilitated trading between southern Arabia and the Mediterranean Sea. Muhammad's father died before he was born and he lost his mother when he was six years old. Two years later his grandfather, who had taken care of him, also died. The young Muhammad was then brought up by his uncle, Abu Talib.

Muhammad worked as a camel-driver and then as a trader, gaining a reputation for honesty in his business dealings. This earned him the nickname 'Al-Amin' (the 'trustworthy one'). Soon he began working for Khadija, a rich widow, and, although Muhammad was 15 years her junior, the two of them married.

> Say – 'We believe in the revelation which has come down to us and also in that which came down to you; our God and your God is one, and it is to Him that we bow.'
>
> QUR'AN, 29.46

God's message

By the time he was 40 years old Muhammad, a deeply religious man, was spending most of his time praying in the desert. He was much troubled by the behaviour of those in Makkah who were worshipping many gods. There were 300 idols of stone, clay and wood in the *Ka'bah* – the shrine in the middle of the city – alone. Muhammad also saw how the rich oppressed the poor, husbands mistreated their wives and children, and gambling and drunkenness were rampant. It was during one of Muhammad's revelations, brought from Allah from the Angel Jibreel in a cave on Mount Hira in 610 CE, that he had a vision. In it he saw a superhuman figure who ordered him to recite a text and called him *Rasul*, the 'messenger of Allah'. The text of this revelation was

A man studies the Qur'an in the mosque at Makkah, the birthplace of Muhammad.

Muhammad was not the founder of Islam and it is offensive to Muslims to refer to their faith as 'Muhammedianism'. The faith of Islam had a divine origin.

There is no God but he.
He gives life, and makes to die.
Believe then in God,
and in his messenger,
the Prophet of the common folk,
who believes in God,
and his words, all who follow him.

QUR'AN, 7.158

later incorporated into the Qur'an (Surah 96).

Deeply disturbed, Muhammad rushed home where his wife and cousin assured him that the message had come from Allah. Many similar visions followed and Muhammad's friends committed them to memory before writing some of them down. Muhammad began preaching the new message to the people of Makkah but few of them responded. It was only when he went to Madinah that his message was welcomed.

Muhammad the Prophet

The people of Madinah, unlike those of Makkah, welcomed Muhammad's message gladly. With their active support he was able to return later to Makkah to cleanse the *Ka'bah* of its idols and dedicate it to the pure worship of Allah.

Muhammad and his early followers were persecuted by the people of Makkah when he told them about his revelations from Allah. The people acted with great brutality, particularly towards the many slaves who had responded to Muhammad's message.

Muhammad's emigration

In 622 Muhammad left Makkah for Madinah in a journey known to all Muslims as the Hijrah ('emigration'). The Muslim calendar is dated from the beginning of the lunar year in which the event took place (AH = 'After Hijrah'). The setting up of a new religious community, known as the Ummah, with Muhammad at its head, took place in Madinah and, as more people responded, Muhammad was welcomed as the ruler of the city. In this religious community the twin principles of equality and freedom were recognized, with Arabs, Jews and other peoples being given equal status. The Ummah became an ideal society based on Muslim principles.

Return to Makkah

All the time he was in Madinah, Muhammad longed to return to Makkah, the city of his birth. In particular, he was desperate to purge the *Ka'bah* of its idols and establish the pure worship of Allah at the shrine. He taught his followers to pray facing in the direction of the shrine, preparing them for the time

Muhammad reacted strongly against all forms of idolatry. Today, any artistic representations of Allah or Muhammad in a mosque are strongly forbidden.

THE DEATH OF MUHAMMAD

Muhammad undertook his last pilgrimage to Makkah in 632 CE. Shortly afterwards he died in Madinah. He was 63 years old and by this time the majority of people in Arabia had accepted the Muslim way of life. He was buried in the house where he died, which by now had become the first Muslim mosque. Although he did not leave a designated successor the mantle of leadership fell to Abu Bakr, his close friend.

when they would return and conquer the city.

His followers won a notable military victory at Badr, in which 300 Muslims defeated 1,000 soldiers from Makkah. This convinced Muhammad and his followers that Allah was on their side.

In March 629 Muhammad entered Makkah, marched seven times around the *Ka'bah* and touched the sacred Black Stone with his staff. He returned to the city in triumph a few months later, to be acclaimed as the Prophet of Allah. The city of Makkah remains at the heart of Islam today.

> *Those of you who worship Muhammad, know that Muhammad is dead. As for those of you who worship God, God is living and will never die. Muhammad is but a messenger; there have been prophets before him, and they all died. Will you turn back?*
>
> ABU BAKR,
> MUHAMMAD'S SUCCESSOR

A muezzin issues the call to prayer from the minaret of a mosque at Lahore in Pakistan.

Two Forms of Islam

There are two groups of Muslim believers. Nine out of every ten are Sunni Muslims while the others are Shi'ites. They disagree over the legitimacy of those who succeeded Muhammad.

After the death of the Prophet Muhammad in 632 there was great concern over who would lead the new religion. Islamic tradition suggests that Muhammad wanted his cousin and son-in-law Shi'at Ali to be his successor. Immediately after the Prophet's death, however, Ali was preoccupied with making the arrangements for his funeral, and some Muslims made Abu Bakr, Muhammad's close friend, the new leader. Abu Bakr was known as the Caliph ('successor') and he was followed by three other close associates of the Prophet who are known by Sunni Muslims as the Four Rightly Guided Caliphs.

This background explains why Islam has been divided into two groups for centuries.

Sunni Muslims

The Sunni make up a large percentage of the Muslim community – the Ummah. Their name is taken from the word *sunnah*, meaning 'path',

> ### SHI'ITE AND SUNNI MUSLIMS
> Shi'ite Islam is the official religion of Iran and the form of Islam followed by Muslim communities in Iraq, India and Pakistan. Elsewhere, Muslim communities are Sunni – from Indonesia (the country with the largest number of Muslims) to Africa, and from Asia to the Arab communities of the Middle East.

referring to the path blazed by Muhammad which was apparent in his words and actions. For Sunni Muslims the Qur'an is fundamental and the *Sunnah* was the first authoritative commentary on the holy book. Sunni Muslims reject the views and customs of various minority groups, representing, as they do, the majority of the Ummah.

Shi'ite Muslims

The Shi'ite Muslims are the true followers of Shi'at Ali, Muhammad's cousin who

The term 'Caliph' was given to Muhammad's designated successor. The Caliph soon became a political leader as well as the defender of the faith. The title was abolished in 1924.

A young priest at theological college in Shiraz, southern Iran. The Shi'ite form of Islam is the official religion of Iran.

eventually became the fourth Caliph. They believe that the guardianship of the legacy bequeathed by Muhammad resided with specific members of his own family, who were appointed by Allah to provide infallible guidance to the Muslim community. These spiritual leaders became known as imams and were thought to be perfect and therefore infallible. Shi'ite Muslims reject the spiritual claims of the first three Caliphs.

In the ninth century a sub-sect of the Shi'ites, the Isma'ilis, appeared in India. This group, headed by the Aga Khan, maintains that there is always an imam directly representing God on earth.

The Qur'an

It is doubtful whether any religious scriptures are read more often or more frequently committed to memory than the Qur'an. To Muslims the Qur'an is the word of God – eternal, absolute and incomparable.

The Arabic word 'Qur'an' means 'recitation' and the full beauty of the holy book can only be appreciated when it is read aloud in the original Arabic, although translations are permitted.

Chapters and verses

The Qur'an refers to itself as the 'preserved tablet' and 'mother of the book'. A single verse in the holy book is called an ayah while each chapter is a surah. There are 114 surahs altogether and all except one begin with the words, 'In the name of Allah – All Gracious, All Merciful…' In Arabic this is known as the *Bismillah* and Muslims usually say it before doing anything of consequence. The surahs are not positioned in the Qur'an in the order in which they were revealed to Muhammad, but that in which they were collected together on the

Malaysian boys reading the Qur'an together. The Qur'an is treated with great respect, and passages are learned by heart and included in prayers.

> *We [God] have revealed the*
> *Qur'an in the Arabic tongue...*
> *This Qur'an could not have been*
> *devised by any but God... It*
> *is beyond doubt from the lord*
> *of the universe.*
> QUR'AN, 12.1; 10.37

orders of the third Caliph, Uthman (644–656).

Each surah is identified by a name taken from some word or subject in it. For instance, the second surah is called 'The Cow' because it relates the story of Moses asking his people to sacrifice a cow. The most familiar surah is the first, however – the *al-Fatihah* – which devout Muslims recite five times a day.

The Qur'an's teaching

Muslims treat the Qur'an with the greatest possible respect, since they believe it is the actual word of God transmitted to the Prophet Muhammad from an original copy preserved in heaven. This divine inspiration and authority applies to all the words in the Arabic original.

The Qur'an teaches all Muslims how to live their lives in total submission to Allah. It also advises them how to prepare themselves for the coming Day of Judgment –

a frequent theme in the holy book – when everyone will stand before Allah and answer for their actions on earth. The eternal destination of all men and women will be decided at that moment – heaven or hell. So that believers can live lives pleasing to Allah they are given advice about a whole range of issues, including the sharing of wealth, the treatment of women and orphans, marriage and divorce, alcohol and gambling, and the lending of money.

As the Qur'an is so highly revered, passages from it are learned by heart and used in prayers. During the holy month of Ramadan, male Muslims set aside time to read the whole book. At Friday Prayers in the mosque the imam uses a passage from the Qur'an as the basis for his sermon, which often carries a political as well as a spiritual message.

The Mosque

Muslims can pray anywhere, but all male Muslims try to be in a mosque for Friday Prayers at noon. The mosque is primarily a place of prayer but it also performs a number of other key functions in the Muslim community.

The mosque acts as a community centre, school and law court for Muslims as well as being a place for prayer. In the early centuries of Islam, Muslims would begin their pilgrimages (Hajj) from the mosque, and it was in the mosque that a Muslim holy war, or jihad, was declared.

Building a mosque
Muhammad promised that anyone involved in building a mosque would pass directly into heaven after death as their actions were so pleasing to Allah. Muhammad built the first mosque in Madinah with his own hands and used the building as his home. All subsequent mosques have been based, as closely as possible, on the pattern established by Muhammad.

The mosque's exterior
Some of the world's most beautiful buildings are mosques, such as the Dome of the Rock in Jerusalem, but most are

The beautifully decorated walls and golden dome of the Dome of the Rock in Jerusalem.

deliberately simple in design. The mosque has two distinguishing features: the dome, representing the universe over which Allah has total control, and four minarets, from which the muezzin intones the call to prayer, or *adhan*, five times a day.

Each Muslim must wash thoroughly before entering the mosque to pray. In Eastern mosques taps are provided in an outside courtyard for the *wudu*, the elaborate washing ritual that always precedes prayer, but in Western mosques these tend to be inside the building.

Inside the mosque

On entering a mosque Muslims remove their shoes and place them in a rack as a sign of respect for Allah. There are no seats in the prayer hall and everyone sits on the heavily patterned carpet which incorporates an arch pointing

Worshippers remove their shoes before entering the prayer hall of a mosque and face in the direction of Makkah to pray.

God is most great, God is most great, God is most great, God is most great. I bear witness that there is no God but Allah, I bear witness that there is no God but Allah. I bear witness that Muhammad is the Prophet of Allah, I bear witness that Muhammad is the Prophet of Allah. Come to prayer. Come to prayer. Come to success. Come to success. God is most great. God is most great. There is no God but Allah.

THE *ADHAN*

FRIDAY PRAYERS

The main weekly service in the mosque is Friday Prayers, which all male Muslims are expected to attend unless they are ill or travelling. At this service the imam leads all worshippers through their prayers and delivers a sermon from a raised platform (the *minbar*). Women are not obliged to attend the mosque for prayers, so rarely do so, but if they do they pray totally separately from the men.

towards Makkah. Many worshippers bring their own prayer mats with them, however. All Muslims must face in the direction of Makkah (qiblah) during prayer. This is indicated by a niche in one wall of the mosque, the *mihrab*. There are no pictures or statues in the mosque, as these are believed to encourage idolatry, but the walls and pillars may be decorated with patterns or verses from the Qur'an in Arabic.

The Five Pillars of Islam

The Five Pillars of Islam are the foundations upon which everything else is built. Tradition describes how Muhammad listed them to a man who asked him about the obligations of being a Muslim.

To a Muslim faith without action is futile since faith motivates action, thus bringing faith out into the real world where it can grow. Islam is a way of life – a mixture of belief, thought and action – and this is reflected in the Five Pillars, the foundations on which the faith is built:

There is no God but Allah, Muhammad is the Messenger of Allah.
THE *SHAHADAH*

◆ The *Shahadah* is the declaration that there is one supreme being, Allah, and that Muhammad is his Prophet. The belief that God is one, so fundamental to Islam, is called the *tawhid*.

◆ *Salah* is prayer. Prayers are said five times a day and are the primary spiritual activity in a Muslim's life.

◆ *Zakah* is the giving of alms to the poor. Because of his poor upbringing Muhammad made looking after

The Qur'an teaches that Allah has 99 beautiful names and these are repeated by Muslims throughout the day. To help them do this without forgetting any they use special prayer beads – *misbeha*.

THE *SHAHADAH*

The *Shahadah*, the declaration of faith in Allah, is the foremost pillar and stands at the heart of the Muslim way of life. It is repeated several times each day, whispered into the ears of newborn babies, taught to every growing child in the *madrassah* (the school in the mosque), and the last words which every Muslim hopes to say before death. Allah was proclaimed by all the prophets before the coming of Muhammad but it was the Prophet who received the final revelation of God. In the Qur'an Allah is the all-powerful one, creator and sustainer of the universe, the controller of all lives and destinies, the merciful and forgiving one, the one who sees and knows all things.

Allah must receive the worship and total loyalty of all Muslims. To express this they say the *Bismillah* ('In the name of Allah') before any significant act and *Inshe Allah* ('God willing') before making any future plans. Nothing happens outside the will of Allah so God's actions must not be questioned – they must be accepted fully.

Clocks showing the times for prayer in a mosque.

the poor and widows a major obligation for all Muslims.

◆ *Sawm* is fasting during the month of Ramadan.

◆ The Hajj is the pilgrimage to the holy places of Islam in Makkah, which should be made once in a lifetime.

A lone worshipper kneels to pray in the mosque of Sokulli Mehmet Paça in Istanbul. There are prescribed positions for prayer, and the words of each prayer are spoken in Arabic.

Prayer

Prayer is so vital that anyone who deliberately avoids praying puts themselves outside the Muslim community. Prayer strengthens the foundations of faith and helps the worshipper to discover real inner peace.

There are two kinds of prayer in Islam. Ritual prayer, or *Salah*, is usually offered in the mosque and only in the Arabic tongue, while private prayer, or *du'a*, may be offered at any time.

Washing, or *wudu*, is an elaborate ritual which always precedes an act of prayer or worship.

Ritual prayer

After the necessary ablutions, or *wudu*, have been offered, *salah* can begin. Muslim tradition prescribes the five times each day when *salah* should be offered: dawn, noon, mid-afternoon, evening and night. *Salah* involves moving through a sequence of actions, often under the

If one of you has a river at his door in which he washes himself five times a day, what do you think? Would it leave any dirt on him? The companions said, 'It would not leave any dirt on him.' The Prophet said, 'This is an example of the five prayers with which Allah blots out the sins of man.'
MUHAMMAD

of day. Each *rak'ah* has the same body movements:

◆ standing with hands to the side in recognition of the lordship of Allah.
◆ standing with thumbs on ear lobes and fingers spread out while reciting the *Shahadah*.
◆ standing with the palm of the right hand resting on the back of the left hand which lies across the chest.
◆ bending from the hips while keeping the back straight and fingers on knees, to express love for Allah while recognizing his greatness and power.
◆ lying prostrate with nose, forehead and the palms of both hands touching the ground – the humblest position offering genuine submission to Allah.
◆ kneeling with the palms of both hands resting on the knees.

In this final position the worshipper meditates for a minute before seeking Allah's forgiveness. Before finishing the *rak'ah* the worshipper looks to the right and to the left to acknowledge the presence of the other worshippers and the unseen guardian angels.

PRIVATE PRAYER

Private prayer, or *du'a*, can be offered to Allah at any time. This may include prayers of thanksgiving, cries for help or prayers for success in a special undertaking.

guidance of an imam, who recites set words from the Qur'an to accompany each action.

Each completed prayer sequence is a *rak'ah* and the number of *rak'ahs* to be performed varies with the time

> Muhammad told his followers that 'a prayer said in congregation' was 27 times more valuable than one said privately.

Muslims at prayer. In some places the mosque is not large enough to accommodate all the worshippers, many of whom pray outside.

Almsgiving and Fasting

Almsgiving and fasting (*zakah* and *sawm*) are the third and fourth of the Five Pillars of Islam.

The third pillar of Islam is to give alms to the poor as a sign of devotion to Allah. The fourth is the discipline of fasting from dawn till dusk during the month of Ramadan.

> *He is not a believer who eats his fill while his neighbour remains hungry by his side.*
>
> MUHAMMAD

Almsgiving

There are two forms of alms-giving:

◆ *Zakah* is a legal requirement stipulating that each Muslim must give 2.5 per cent of their wealth to charity each year. In Muslim countries this is collected by the government and distributed to the poor while elsewhere each Muslim must make their own arrangements for paying it and deciding how it will be spent. Every Muslim knows that Allah will hold them accountable on the Day of Judgment for their honesty and integrity in money matters.

◆ *Sadaqah* is a voluntary donation which can be given to charity at any time. This donation should preferably be handed over in secret and does not affect the compulsory *zakah*.

After *salah*, *zakah* is the foremost spiritual duty of Muslims. All giving should be generous; there is no upper limit since wealth is a gift from Allah. By giving freely a person 'purifies' their wealth and prevents their soul from depending on material possessions rather than on Allah. To those receiving help *zakah* is not charity as every

Compulsory donations (*zakah*) are collected outside a mosque. The amount given is a 40th of a person's annual income and is generally distributed to the poor and needy.

member of the Muslim community has the God-given right to share in the beneficence and goodness of Allah.

Fasting

The fourth pillar specifies that all healthy Muslims must fast during the daylight hours of Ramadan, the ninth month in the Muslim calendar, and this includes abstinence from sexual intercourse as well as from food and drink. No smoking is allowed either and toothpaste cannot be used. The only people not included are children (who are introduced to fasting gradually), the sick, the elderly, nursing or pregnant women and travellers. Those travelling during Ramadan are under a spiritual obligation to carry out the full fast later on.

The Ramadan fast is vital to the worldwide Muslim community since it binds individuals together in the Ummah. Those who have never known hunger share the daily experience of their poor brothers and sisters. Fasting also gives a believer more time to concentrate on Allah, to pray with more intensity, to give more generously and to read the whole Qur'an. During Ramadan, worshippers draw a little closer to the angels, who always behave perfectly in Allah's presence.

The Qur'an tells Muslims that, during Ramadan, they can eat and drink until they can distinguish a white thread from a black one in the light of the coming dawn. They should then fast until nightfall when they cannot tell them apart.

OTHER GUIDELINES

The Qur'an forbids Muslims to be money-lenders or behave unethically. The holy book also gives clear guidelines about marriage and divorce, inheritance and property rights, and the treatment of women and slaves along with suitable codes of dress. In matters of clothing, Islam considers anything which gives a false impression, or reflects pride, to be wrong. The Qur'an stipulates that women should dress to cover their bodies, and the clothing should be neither light nor transparent. A similar directive is given to men.

Pilgrimage

The pilgrimage to Makkah, or Hajj, is one of the world's great annual religious events. Every healthy Muslim is obliged to make the pilgrimage once in his or her lifetime.

The fifth and final duty of every healthy Muslim is to make a pilgrimage (the Hajj) to the holy shrine of the *Ka'bah* in Makkah. Before they can do so, however, they must provide adequately for their family and other dependants while they are away. The pilgrimage is only possible between the 8th and 13th days of Dhul-Hijjah, the last month in the Islamic year.

The Hajj
On the outskirts of Makkah each male pilgrim dons two identical white unsewn cloths (*ihram*). This shows that everyone, whatever their wealth, is equal before Allah. They then wash thoroughly and make a declaration of their intention to complete the Hajj successfully. From now on they must abstain from shaving any part of their body, cutting their nails, using any oil or perfume, having sexual intercourse, plucking grass or cutting down trees. This puts the pilgrim in a fit state of mind to successfully complete the Hajj.

On reaching the city each pilgrim, following the example of the Prophet Muhammad on his last visit to the city, walks anticlockwise seven times around the *Ka'bah*. This is called the *tawaf*. Three circuits are completed quickly then, during the fourth, each pilgrim pauses to touch or kiss the Black Stone in the south-west corner of the *Ka'bah*. As the *Ka'bah*, the House of Allah, is the focus of all Muslim devotion, the Black Stone is the holiest object in Islam.

Pilgrims then run between the twin hills of Safa and Mawa to remind them of Hajar's frantic search for water for her young son, Isma'il, before she discovered a well (the well of Zamzam) provided by God. Many pilgrims take a small phial of this water back home with them after the Hajj.

Muhammad delivered his last sermon from the Mount of Mercy in 632. Here, each pilgrim stands before Allah in meditation from noon to sunset.

Pilgrims walk around the *Ka'bah* in Makkah. The *Ka'bah* contains the Black Stone, which Muslims believe was given by the Angel Jibreel to Adam. It was later put into the wall of the *Ka'bah* by Abraham.

Each year more than two million pilgrims undertake the Hajj. A male who completes the pilgrimage is called a hajji and a woman a hajjah. Many hajjis keep their pilgrimage clothes so they can be buried in them.

The pilgrims then go to the village of Mina where there are three stone pillars representing Iblis, the devil. Pilgrims throw seven stones at each pillar as a reminder that Isma'il was tempted by Iblis to run away three times when Ibrahim was about to sacrifice him. After this animals are sacrificed.

Then there is a four-day festival, which is celebrated by Muslims throughout the world – the festival of *Id-ul-Adha*. A final circuit of the *Ka'bah* back in Makkah, the discarding of the *ihram* and a haircut for male pilgrims mark the end of the Hajj. While the majority of pilgrims return home after the Hajj, some travel on to Madinah to visit Muhammad's tomb.

From Birth to Death

In line with other religions, Islam marks each momentous stage in life – birth, marriage and death – with both private and public ceremonies.

All babies born into Muslim families are considered to be gifts from Allah, so they are welcomed by the Ummah – the worldwide Muslim community. Within minutes of birth the father takes the infant into his arms and whispers the *Shahadah* into its right ear to make sure that he or she hears the name of Allah before anything else. An elderly relative places a small piece of sugar or date on the baby's tongue to express the hope that he or she will grow up to be sweet natured and generous.

Seven days later the baby's head is shaved and gold or silver equivalent to the weight of the hair is given to the poor in the *aqiqah* ceremony. At the same time the child is given its names with one being taken from Allah or Muhammad. Many Muslim boys are circumcised at the same time, although this can be left until much later.

Then, when the child is four years, four months and four days old, his or her religious education begins. For

> *God fixes the time span for all things… it is he who causes people to die and to be born; it is he who caused male and female; it is he who will re-create us anew.*
> QUR'AN, 75.3–4

A Muslim father whispers the *Shahadah* into the ear of his newborn child.

school in the mosque – the *madrassah*.

Marriage

Muslims consider the family to be the foundation of society and marriage the backbone of family life. In Muslim communities the whole family is involved in the choice of a marriage partner and, when an arrangement has been made, a dowry is paid by the bridegroom or his father. This is an important safeguard for the bride, who is unlikely to earn money of her own. In the marriage ceremony a contract between groom and bride is signed in the presence of two male witnesses.

A Muslim burial in Iran. Muslims never cremate bodies, because they believe death will be followed by a bodily resurrection and the Day of Judgment.

the *Bismillah* ceremony the child learns the first line of the first surah in the Qur'an (the *al-Fatihah*), to commemorate the time when the Angel Jibreel first appeared to Muhammad. From this time until adulthood the child's religious education will continue regularly at the

Muslim tradition teaches that two angels visit the grave and question the dead person about their fitness for the next life. The *Shahadah* and the *al-Fatihah* are recited over the grave so that the dead person knows how to answer the angels.

FUNERALS

Muslims believe strongly in the resurrection of the body and life after death so they approach death hopefully. A dying person recites the *Shahadah* while relatives read passages from the Qur'an around the bed. Then, after death, the body is washed three times, wrapped in three white sheets and carried on a stretcher to the place of burial. The corpse is laid directly on the soil, resting on its right side with the head turned to face Makkah. The mourners recite the *al-Fatihah* before returning home. On the first Friday after the funeral family members may visit the grave and leave a palm leaf – a symbol of peace.

The Muslim Way of Life

Eating with thankfulness the pure and wholesome food provided by Allah is an act of worship in itself. Certain substances are forbidden, however, such as pork and alcohol, since they carry individual and social dangers.

M ost food is lawful for Muslims and following a moderate and healthy diet is a religious as well as a physical necessity. The Qur'an, however, does introduce certain restrictions.

Lawful and unlawful food
Muslims must only eat halal

Bedouin men share a meal in Bahrain. Strict laws define which foods Muslims may eat, and alcohol is never permitted.

food (that permitted according to Islamic laws) and not touch haram (forbidden) food. According to the Qur'an, haram food includes any meat from an animal that has been killed in an unknown way, or which still contains blood; the flesh of any animal that has died rather than having been slaughtered; any pig meat, since pigs live off rotting foods and offal; and meat from any animal that has

> *'O ye who believe!' Eat of the good things we have provided for you and be grateful to God if it is him you worship.*
>
> QUR'AN, 2.173

> *Tell believing women to avert their glances and guard their private parts, and not to display their charms except that [which normally] appears to them.*
>
> QUR'AN, 24.30

been slaughtered in a name other than Allah's.

If the choice is between eating forbidden food and starving, however, then a Muslim can eat anything with a clear conscience.

Even lawful food must be prepared under strict conditions before it is suitable to eat, and all animals must be slaughtered with compassion. Their throats must be cut with the sharpest possible knife, to bring death quickly and relatively painlessly, while the *Bismillah* blessing is pronounced. The death of one animal should not be witnessed by another.

Alcohol

According to the Qur'an the date palm and vine provide fresh fruits, date honey and vinegar. Yet the intoxicants which destabilize individuals and communities come from rotting, fermented fruits. This shows that, while Allah has provided everything in nature for us to enjoy, he does allow Iblis (Satan) to tempt us away from the straight path through a misuse of these gifts. Drinking alcohol is a prime example of this and therefore to be avoided.

Islam Today

Islam is the fastest growing religion in the modern world. As the religion expands it becomes more powerful in world affairs so gaining even more converts.

Over recent centuries Islam has become increasingly influential on a global scale. Many of the newly emerging Third World countries in the 20th century were Muslim. Some of these are central to the world's economy as they control crucial supplies of natural gas, oil and minerals.

A growing religion

Islam is expanding throughout the world. There are now over 1,000 million Muslims in the Middle East, Africa, India, Central Asia and other regions of the world. The largest Muslim community is found in Indonesia, where 186 million Muslims form over 90 per cent of the total population. There are also large indigenous communities in Eastern Europe – particularly in Albania, Macedonia and the southern states of the former USSR. Sizeable Muslim communities are found in Western Europe, too, especially in Italy, Germany and the Netherlands. Five per

Islam is broad enough to create works of art of outstanding beauty and willingly embrace new developments in science and technology at the same time.

The death penalty is mandatory for apostasy that is committed by any Muslim who advocates apostasy from Islam or openly declares his [or her] own apostasy by their own actions.

SUDAN PENAL CODE, 1991

The three biggest Muslim countries in terms of land mass are Sudan, Algeria and Saudi Arabia. Each of these is about the size of all the countries of Europe put together.

cent of the French population is Muslim.

It is thought that Islam will soon become the second largest religion in the USA after Christianity. Sixty per cent of American Muslims are immigrants from the Middle East and 40 per cent are converts – mostly African-Americans.

Muslims now make up the majority of people in 30 countries in the world. In many more areas, such as Nigeria,

India, the Philippines and north-west China, they comprise a significant proportion of the population. Islam is the major religion in both some of the richest and some of the poorest countries of the world – with Saudi Arabia at one end of the spectrum and Sudan and Bangladesh at the other.

Sikhism is the newest of the world's religions. In the Sikh Gurdwara Act, passed in India in 1925, a Sikh was defined as: 'one who believes in the 10 Gurus and the *Guru Granth Sahib* and is not a *patit* [lapsed member]'. As this still left room for some confusion a meeting convened in Amritsar in North India in 1931 defined true Sikh belief and practice. In future a Sikh would be recognized as someone who has faith in one God, the teachings of the 10 Gurus and the *Adi Granth*; who believes in the importance and necessity of *amrit*; who does not belong to any other religion; and who is a member of a Sikh community, accepting the discipline of that community.

Although Sikhism started in India (in the region which is now Pakistan)

The Golden Temple at Amritsar, North India, is surrounded by the Lake of Immortality. Pilgrims reach it via a marble causeway.

Sikhs are now scattered throughout the world. The largest community outside India is in Britain, where there are some 500,000 Sikhs. Sikhism is still firmly rooted in the culture of India, however, and stresses the importance of personal appearance and hygiene in the service of God.

Listen my heart, love God ceaselessly,
as the fish loves the water.
The deeper the water the happier
and the more tranquil the fish,
The greatest sickness of the soul is this,
to forget for even a second the Beloved.
ADI GRANTH

SIKHISM

Contents

The Founder of Sikhism

Sikhism was founded by Guru Nanak, who respected both Hinduism and Islam but believed they obscured the truth about God. Sikhism stresses an individual's personal relationship with the divine.

Born in 1469 in Talwindi, now Nankana Sahib, in modern Pakistan, Guru Nanak came from a prosperous Hindu background. As a young child he soon displayed outstanding qualities of wisdom and spiritual insight, and his teachers soon decided there was little they could teach him. He spent much of his early life talking to travelling Hindu and Muslim holy men.

In accordance with Hindu custom Nanak's marriage was arranged by his father when he was 18. However, when Nanak's first child was born, he refused to perform the

The first and last of the 10 Sikh Gurus. Guru Nanak, the founder of Sikhism (left), with the last and next most important Guru, Guru Gobind Singh.

> *There is neither Hindu nor Muslim so whose path shall I follow? I shall follow God's path. God is neither Hindu nor Muslim and the path which I follow is God's.*
> GURU NANAK (1469–1539), THE FOUNDER OF SIKHISM

Receiving God's call

At the age of 30 Nanak had a spiritual experience that changed the course of his life. While he was bathing in the River Bein he felt himself being carried up into the heavenly court and taken before God, where he was given a cup of nectar, or *amrit*, to drink. The people who knew him were sure that he had drowned but he returned to them three days later and announced that God had called him to be a Guru.

For the next 20 years Nanak travelled throughout India and the adjoining Muslim countries, visiting all the holy places of Hinduism and Islam to preach. Then he settled down as a farmer with his family in the Punjab. Gradually, a community of disciples, or Sikhs, grew up around him. A few days before his death in 1539, Guru Nanak nominated his most devoted follower, Lehna, to succeed him.

usual Hindu rituals to remove the child's impurities. Birth, he said, was a natural event and the real impurities were 'the covetous mind, tongues speaking untruths, eyes full of lust, and ears accepting unreliable evidence as true'.

GURU NANAK'S MESSAGE

The message that Guru Nanak preached cut across many cherished Hindu and Muslim beliefs while reinforcing others. He told the people that:

◆ there is one God who is both with them in the world, and yet over and above that world.

◆ there is a continual cycle of birth, life, death and rebirth, through which everyone must pass.

◆ the goal of each person's soul is to finally be reabsorbed into the God from whom they originally came.

◆ those who hope to return to God must discipline themselves and live by certain moral principles. Above all else they must live humbly and be at the constant service of others.

The 10 Gurus

The 10 Gurus, beginning with Guru Nanak, make up an unbroken line of revelation from God. Each Guru was chosen by his predecessor and each possessed the same knowledge about God.

Guru Nanak had two sons and they were not pleased when he chose one of his disciples, Lehna, to succeed him. On many occasions Guru Nanak set his sons menial tasks to test their spiritual suitability for leadership, but they had invariably considered such chores beneath them. Lehna, though, had been set the same challenges and had responded immediately.

> *The whole world enjoys the sight of the Guru. But none will be saved by the mere sight of him. One must mould one's thoughts according to the Guru's words.*
>
> GURU AMAR DAS,
> THE THIRD GURU

Guru Nanak's successors

On Guru Nanak's death Lehna became Guru Angad, the second Guru (1539–52). He developed Gurmukhi, the language in which the Sikh scriptures are written, and this allowed Sikhism to develop an identity of its own. Guru Angad also wrote hymns in the new language, always including Nanak's name in the last line.

Guru Amar Das (1552–74), the third Guru, made a significant contribution to Sikhism when he built the first open kitchen, or langar, so that everyone visiting him could eat together first. This taught every visitor the all-important lesson that everyone is equal in the sight of God – a central Sikh belief. The langar remains an important feature in the spiritual life of every Sikh temple, or gurdwara (the 'door of the Guru'), today.

Guru Ram Das (1574–81), the fourth Guru, is best known for founding the holy city of Amritsar in North India, but he also wrote the hymn on which every Sikh wedding ceremony is based and this meant that Sikhs no longer needed to make use of the Hindu scriptures and priests.

It was Guru Arjan (1581–1606), the fifth Guru, who built a beautiful temple, the *Harimandir*, in the middle of an artificial lake in Amritsar –

According to the Sikh faith it was God alone who inspired the human Gurus and the *Guru Granth Sahib*. For this reason God is called the true Guru, or *Sat Guru*.

Young Sikhs with swords and turbans. Persecution of Sikhs, by the Indian Mughal empire (1526–1857) and by Hindu kings, led Guru Gobind Singh to sanction the use of force to achieve justice and religious freedom.

later to become the Golden Temple. Guru Arjan also brought together the hymns written by the early Gurus, added some of his own and published them as the *Adi Granth* – the 'first book'. This was later known as the *Guru Granth Sahib*. In the following year Guru Arjan became the first Sikh martyr.

and Guru Tegh Bahadur (1664–75) then followed.

The 10th Guru

By the time of Guru Gobind Singh (1675–1708), the 10th and last human Guru, there had been torture, repression and death of many followers. He believed it expedient to turn the faith into a fighting force

His successor, Guru Har Gobind (1606–44), carried two swords, symbolizing battle and the spirit. Physical and spiritual elements have been combined in Sikhism ever since.

Guru Har Rai (1644–61), Guru Har Krishan (1661–64)

so that, if necessary, it could defend itself. It was for this reason that he established the Khalsa, the Sikh brotherhood.

The Sikh Community

Formed in 1699 by Guru Gobind Singh as a militant brotherhood to defend Sikhism, the Khalsa now unites both male and female Sikhs in upholding their faith through serving the community and each other.

In 1699, Guru Gobind Singh (then called Guru Gobind Rai), the 10th Guru, called all Sikhs together for the April festival of Baisakhi. Sword in hand he asked for volunteers who would be willing to die for their faith. One man disappeared with the Guru into his tent and the Guru reappeared carrying a bloodstained sword. Four other men then followed suit, with the same outcome. All Sikhs pay tribute to the courage of these five men – the Five Faithful Ones or the *panj piares*.

The *panj piares* became the first members of the Khalsa (the 'pure ones'). As part of their initiation they were given *amrit* to drink. This was prepared in an iron bowl using water and sugar crystals, as it is today, and stirred with a two-edged sword, or *khanda*. After this, the Guru himself became a member of the Khalsa and changed his name to Guru Gobind Singh.

The code of discipline

Guru Gobind Singh laid down a strict code of discipline which every member of the Khalsa still follows today. They recite five hymns each day; they do not drink alcohol or take drugs; they must not steal, commit adultery or gamble; they must serve all members of humanity, especially the poor; and they must be willing to serve God, the true

Joining the fraternity

Men who become members of the Khalsa take on the surname Singh ('lion') and women the surname Kaur ('princess'). Joining the fraternity is a 'baptism by the sword' and this has been the focus for Sikh unity since Guru Gobind Singh's time. The ideals of the Khalsa are very precious to its members, and all decisions are made in the presence of the 11th Guru – the *Guru Granth Sahib*.

Guru, in any way necessary. In addition all members of the Khalsa must wear the Five Ks:

A Sikh with the distinctive unshorn beard, sword and steel bracelet of a Khalsa member.

◆ *Kesh* is unshorn beard and uncut hair – signs of holiness and dedication to God.
◆ *Kirpan* is a sword, symbolizing the willingness

He who repeats night and day the name of God whose enduring light is unquenchable. He who bestows not a thought on any but the one God. He who has full love and confidence in God... He who recognizes only the one God... In whose heart the light of the perfect One shines, he is recognized as a pure member of the Khalsa.

GURU GOBIND SINGH,
THE 10TH GURU

that God is one and that the link between God and the worshipper is unbreakable.
◆ *Kachera* are traditional shorts, worn to show that the person is always ready to defend Sikhism.

to fight against physical and spiritual oppression.
◆ *Kangha* is a comb, essential for basic cleanliness, one of the foundations of Sikhism.
◆ *Kara* is a steel bracelet worn on the right wrist as a reminder

Beliefs

For Sikhs the ultimate goal of human existence is
the restoration of the human soul to unity with God.
This can be brought closer by spiritual activity and
discipline but it can only be finally achieved through
the grace of God.

The different aspects of
Sikh belief are closely
intertwined.

God

The first verse in the *Guru
Granth Sahib* is the foundation
of all Sikh religion and is
known as the *Mool Mantar*. It
shows that God is unknowable,
without form, without
qualities and beyond
description. It follows from
this that God cannot take a
human form. Yet the word of
God, expressed by the Gurus
and especially the *Guru Granth
Sahib*, is God present in the
world, especially in the depths
of the human soul.

> There is only one God, whose
> name is Truth. Who is the
> all-pervading Creator, without
> fear, without time, without form.
> He is beyond birth and death, he
> is self-enlightened. He is known
> by the Grace of the Guru.
>
> THE *MOOL MANTAR*

The search for truth

Sikhism stresses a highly
personal relationship with God
through inwardly reactivating
the divine spark which is in
every soul. Each person must
discover God for themselves –
there are no priests in Sikhism
to act as intermediaries. Guru
Nanak told his followers to
look for the truth which is

REINCARNATION

Sikhism retains a belief in reincarnation and
karma. It is only by meditating on God's
name, and by serving others, that release
from the cycle of birth, life and death can
be achieved. Good karma means rebirth as a
human being but bad karma leads to rebirth as
an animal. To focus one's entire being on God
is to be a *gurmukh* and put oneself in the way
of God's grace. This is the only way to go
beyond reincarnation to liberation and
enlightenment. The place of liberation is
nirvana, a restoration of the unity that the
soul once enjoyed with God, and this can be
brought closer by congregating with other
believers, singing hymns and praying.

During a Sikh wedding the couple will walk a number of times around the *Guru Granth Sahib*, accompanied by their families as a gesture of support.

Sikhism sees men and women as equals, and also works to break down class distinctions. Both men and women can officiate at Sikh ceremonies.

God's name in their hearts and minds. Sikhs do this by repeating that name over and over again, morning and night. Guru Nanak called God *Nam* ('name') or *Sat Guru* ('true Guru'). When a person meditates continually upon *Nam* they are bringing the essence of God into their lives.

behind all religion, and Sikhs identify truth with God.

The *langar*, where everyone eats the same food together, reinforces the teaching of the *Guru Granth Sahib* that all human beings, men and women, are equal. The Sikh scriptures express the same truth, by including hymns from Hindu and Muslim holy men.

Guru Nanak taught that people should always keep

Scriptures

Any room in which the *Guru Granth Sahib* is installed is called a gurdwara. The scriptures are treated with the same care as any of the 10 human Gurus.

The *Guru Granth Sahib*, the 'book of the Guru', stands at the heart of Sikh worship and belief. It occupies a special raised 'throne' (the *takht*) under a canopy in the gurdwara. The *granthi*, an official of the gurdwara, is entrusted with taking care of the holy book, and makes sure that it receives due respect by waving a *chauri*, a fan of yak-tail hair, over it. When the *Guru Granth Sahib* is too old to be

The Guru Granth Sahib is honoured in the same way that the 10 human Gurus were. The reader waves the sacred fan, or chauri, over the book, giving it the attention a living Guru would receive in a hot climate.

Each copy of the *Guru Granth Sahib* must be identical. Each one is 1,430 pages long with exactly the same layout.

used it is cremated and its ashes are scattered on a local river – a ceremony befitting any human Guru.

The *Japji Sahib*

The key to the *Guru Granth Sahib*, and to all Sikh teaching, is the *Japji Sahib*. It forms the first section of the holy book and was written by Guru Nanak

> *So pure is God's Name, whoever obeys God knows the pleasure of it in his own heart.*
>
> JAPJI SAHIB

towards the end of his life. It is the only hymn which is spoken and not sung. It is recited each morning by devout Sikhs and during the preparation of the *amrit* for initiation into the Khalsa.

The *Japji Sahib*, commencing with the *Mool Mantar*, underlines the most fundamental Sikh beliefs:

◆ There is but one God who is eternal truth.
◆ A cycle of rebirth governs human existence with karma deciding the next rebirth.
◆ Salvation can only be reached after a person meditates on God, repeats the divine name and serves others.

THE 11TH GURU

The *Guru Granth Sahib* was originally an anthology called the *Adi Granth*, compiled in 1604 by Guru Arjan. This book was placed in the *Harimandir*, the Golden Temple, in Amritsar.

Guru Gobind Singh, the last human Guru, declared that the holy book was the 11th and last Guru and gave the book its final form. The hymns and poems in the *Guru Granth Sahib* are placed in 31 divisions, each beginning with the *Mool Mantar*, which is sung at morning and evening services in the gurdwara. Guru Arjan contributed the most hymns (2,218), followed by Guru Nanak (974), then Guru Amar Das (907).

The Temple

The temple, or gurdwara, is the main place of worship for all Sikhs. A copy of the *Guru Granth Sahib* must be installed in the building if it is to be recognized as a gurdwara.

Sikhs are encouraged to worship together since this unites the community. Guru Nanak taught the value of congregation, saying it is by associating with those who are good that one becomes good. A gurdwara is easily recognizable due to the yellow flag – the *Nishan Sahib* – flying outside. The flag depicts a two-edged sword, the *khanda*, representing the struggle against the physical and spiritual enemies of the faith. The two swords, or *kirpans*, stand for the authority of the 10 Gurus, while the circle represents the unity of God.

The Sikh flag, the *Nishan Sahib*, always flies outside the gurdwara. It is replaced with a different flag during the New Year festival.

Inside a gurdwara

The gurdwara is considered holy ground, so Sikhs cover their heads – men with turbans and women with silk scarves – and remove their shoes before entering. The main room, or *diwan*, contains the *Guru Granth Sahib*, which is raised up on cushions and covered by a canopy. This is a reminder that the 10 human Gurus taught their followers from an elevated position. Each night five *granthis* carry the holy book above their heads to a separate room.

Otherwise the *diwan* is bare with no seats, although there may be paintings of various Gurus on the walls. The people attending the services sit cross-legged on the floor, underlining the teaching that everyone is equal in God's sight and is under the authority of the *Guru Granth Sahib* while inside the gurdwara.

The original gurdwaras were modest in appearance, so as not to attract the unwelcome attention of Muslim rulers, and most gurdwaras remain simple in design. In India they are open from dawn till dusk

specially trained to read Gurmukhi – the language of the *Guru Granth Sahib*.

> *The company of those who cherish the true Lord who is within turns mortals into godly people…*
> *Man becomes good in good company. It helps him to pursue virtue and cleanses him of vices.*
>
> ADI GRANTH

A gurdwara service with the *Guru Granth Sahib* enthroned on cushions underneath a canopy. The service consists of readings and interpretations, hymns and offerings. Worshippers are free to come and go at any time during the proceedings.

and worshippers can enter them at any time to listen to a reading from the *Guru Granth Sahib* or pray. Anyone can read from the holy book, but larger gurdwaras employ a *granthi*

Worship

The gurdwara is where the *sadhsangat*, the Sikh congregation, meets daily for the *kirtan*, the devotional singing of hymns from the *Guru Granth Sahib*. This activity forms the basis of all Sikh worship.

Worshippers gather together in the gurdwara on the most convenient day, which is usually Sunday. Having washed thoroughly at home, the worshippers pause outside the gurdwara to touch the flagpole and the step before touching their foreheads with the same hand.

The service in the gurdwara can last for several hours and it provides an opportunity for reading and meditating on the words of the *Guru Granth Sahib*. Although Sikhs may have their own copy of the holy book at home, many cannot meet the requirement that it be kept in an upstairs room on its own, so they make the most of this opportunity to study it.

A key point in the service is when the *Guru Granth Sahib* is

Music plays an important part in Sikh worship. When Guru Nanak was asked a question, his reply was often in the form of a song.

A COMMUNAL MEAL

After the service everyone eats a communal meal in the *langar*. This practice was instituted by Guru Nanak and endorsed by his successors. Any Sikh can help to prepare the food, which is always vegetarian to avoid offending anyone. The symbolic value of the *langar* in the Sikh community is considerable as an open demonstration that everyone is treated equally in the presence of God – a fundamental Sikh belief.

The Sikh ideal of equality is demonstrated in the *langar*, where everyone is welcome to eat, irrespective of caste or status. Each person contributes according to his ability, and takes according to his need. All members of the community take a turn in preparing and serving food.

opened at random and a passage is read out, beginning at the top left-hand corner of the page. This reading is known as the will of God, or the *hukam*.

The service ends with the *Anand* of Guru Ram Das, the epilogue of Guru Nanak's *Japji Sahib*, a verse from a hymn by Guru Arjan and the *Ardas* – a prayer which is said by a member of the congregation. The final *hukam* leaves each worshipper with a thought from God to carry with them into the coming week.

A holy meal

After the service, everyone eats *karah parshad* in the *langar*. This 'holy food' is prepared before the service and is stirred with a *kirpan* as it ends. The sweetness of the holy food, a mixture of wheat flour, butter, sugar and water, reminds everyone of the sweetness of God. It is shared among all the people, including non-Sikhs, showing that no one leaves God's house hungry.

> *Wherever my Sat Guru [God]*
> *goes and sits, that place is*
> *beautiful, O Lord King. The*
> *Guru's disciples seek their*
> *place and take and apply*
> *its dust to their foreheads.*
> ADI GRANTH

Festivals and Celebrations

The three main Sikh festivals — Baisakhi, Divali and *Hola Mohalla* — are borrowed from Hinduism. The primary celebrations are *gurpurbs*, which commemorate events in the lives of the Gurus.

The first Sikh festivals were introduced by Guru Amar Das, while Guru Gobind Singh added the Hindu festival of *Holi*, which Sikhs know as *Hola Mohalla*. These three festivals are now known as *melas* — 'fairs'. Today, however, *gurpurbs* are the most widely observed celebrations, rejoicing over the lives of the 10 Gurus.

New Year festival

Baisakhi, celebrated on 13 April, is the beginning of the Sikh New Year and, in the Punjab, coincides with the spring wheat harvest. Worldwide, Sikhs link it with the inauguration of the Khalsa and, because of this, Baisakhi is the traditional time for joining the brotherhood. The *Nishan Sahib*, the symbol of Sikh presence in the community that flies outside each gurdwara, is replaced with a different flag at Baisakhi.

Festival of lights

Divali is the festival of lights during which gurdwaras are brightly lit to celebrate the coming of light into the natural world as well as symbolizing the inner light which directs the believer towards union with God.

THE *AKHAND* PATH

The centrepiece of a *gurpurb* is the *Akhand* Path. This is a continuous reading of the whole of the *Guru Granth Sahib* by a relay of people. The entire reading lasts about 48 hours and its completion coincides with the beginning of the *gurpurb*. At page 1426 a special ceremony begins, involving reading from here to the end of the holy book, then the *Japji*, six verses of the *Anand Sahib*, the *Ardas* prayer and the distribution of *karah parshad*. Everyone shares a meal during the readings.

Khalsa members lead a procession to dedicate a temple in Kenya.

The festival of *Hola Mohalla*

Hola Mohalla ('attack or be attacked') celebrates the

> *Non-Sikh festivals should not be celebrated. Even if we do observe the same day we do it in our own way.*
>
> GURU AMAR DAS,
> THE THIRD GURU

military prowess of the worldwide Sikh community with mock battles taking place in and around Anandpur, in the Punjab. Traditional Sikh warriors compete in wrestling, archery and shooting competitions.

Gurpurbs

Gurpurbs commemorate the births and deaths of the 10 Gurus. Three *gurpurbs* are celebrated by Sikhs worldwide – the birthdays of Guru Nanak and Guru Gobind Singh and the martyrdom of Guru Arjan.

Amritsar

Although Guru Nanak saw no value in undertaking a spiritual pilgrimage, many Sikhs travel to see the Golden Temple in Amritsar. This is the centre of Sikhism and the scene of continual acts of worship and readings from the *Guru Granth Sahib*.

The *Harimandir*, the central building of the Golden Temple complex.

When Sikhism was founded there were 68 places of Hindu pilgrimage but Guru Nanak did not attach importance to any of them. He taught his followers to search for a knowledge of God through contemplation and worship, rather than by association with any holy place. The city of Amritsar ('the pool of nectar'), in North India, was founded in 1577 by Guru Ram Das who built a brick temple there. The site was surrounded by a sacred lake and this was extended by Guru Arjan.

The Golden Temple

Along the causeway, in the middle of the lake, is the beautiful Golden Temple (*Harimandir*) with verses from the *Adi Granth* inscribed on the façade. The temple has four entrances – unlike Hindu temples and Muslim mosques – symbolizing the belief that God's house is open to members of all castes. Instead of going up into the building, the worshipper descends into the Golden Temple to demonstrate the humbling of him or herself before God.

Inside the temple there are pictures of Guru Nanak with his Hindu and Muslim disciples. Each morning five Sikhs carry the *Guru Granth Sahib* on their shoulders in a

View through the gateway (right) of the Golden Temple. Above this gateway is a treasury containing four sets of golden doors, jewelled canopies and the golden spades that were used to dig the pool.

If a man goes to bathe at a place of pilgrimage with the mind of a crook and the body of a thief his exterior will of course be washed by bathing but his interior will become sullied twice over. He will be cleaned from without like a gourd but he will be cherishing pure poison within. The saints are good even without such ablutions. The thief remains a thief even if he bathes thus at the places of pilgrimage.

ADI GRANTH

silver casket along the causeway to the Golden Temple. Here they place it on a cushion beneath a canopy. During the daylight hours verses are read continually from the holy book. Then, at nightfall, it is returned to the treasury where it is guarded until the following day.

At the beginning of the 19th century Maharajah Ranjit Singh rebuilt the temple in Amritsar in marble, covered it with gilded copper and inlaid it with semi-precious stones. From then on it was known as the Golden Temple.

Sikhism Today

Although Sikhism has spread throughout the world, most notably to North America and Britain, it is still very much associated with its birthplace in the Punjab.

B y the beginning of the 19th century Sikh religious values in India had largely been overtaken by the dominant Hindu culture. As the century drew to a close, however, the work of Hindu and Christian missionaries in the Punjab forced the Sikhs to go on the offensive. Small groups were established to educate Sikhs in their faith and schools were set up in which the *Guru Granth Sahib* played a key role. The Sikh Gurdwara Act of 1925 placed the responsibility for looking after Sikh shrines in the hands of a committee. The committee decided that Sikhism had long been diluted by its close ties with Hinduism and it led a movement back to 'pure' Sikhism.

Sikhism as a world religion

In 1947 the Punjab, the Sikh homeland, was divided and 2,600,000 Sikhs moved into India from the part of the Punjab controlled by Pakistan. Although 80 per cent of Sikhs still live in the Punjab they began to see their faith as a

A strong community spirit characterizes Sikhism. Here men and women work together in building a temple.

worldwide, and not just a local, religion. Many Sikhs left their homeland to settle in the USA and the community there now numbers some 350,000. Although not normally a missionary religion a feature of the American community is the number of 'white (*gora*) Sikhs'. These converts have adopted the Punjabi clothes and lifestyle, having their children educated along Sikh lines.

Sikh men came to Britain looking for work, leaving women and children behind until they had established themselves. The vast majority settled in and around the large cities; major communities were set up in London, Birmingham, Leicester and West Yorkshire. To meet the spiritual and social needs of these communities over 150 gurdwaras have been opened. Although the first British Sikh gurdwara was opened in 1911 the main influx of Sikhs took place in the 1950s and early 1960s. The Sikh community now numbers about 500,000.

Such communities faced, and continue to face, many problems. Many Sikhs have discarded elements of their traditional way of life which

Truth is the highest of all virtues but higher still is truthful living.
ADI GRANTH

marked them out as distinctive – their long hair, turbans and beards among them. Conflicts between the generations have arisen, in particular over the tradition of arranged marriages. Religious differences have been aired over whether services in the gurdwaras should continue to be conducted in Punjabi or in the vernacular language of most worshippers. Certainly fewer and fewer Sikhs outside the Punjab are learning the language of their ancestors and this leads to less respect being given to the *Guru Granth Sahib*.

Candles are used by many religions as symbols of light shining in the dark.

OTHER WORLD FAITHS

Confucianism

The teaching of Confucius has formed the mainstream of Chinese philosophy for the past 2,000 years. Despite decades of Communist rule and the Cultural Revolution (1966–69) its influence in China remains considerable.

Strictly speaking, Confucianism is not a religion but a code of ethics, a way of living here on earth. This moral code was laid down by Kung Fu-Tzu (c. 551–479 BCE), better known in the West as Confucius.

Teachings

Confucius taught that heaven and earth would be in harmony if everyone obeyed those above them and dealt justly with those below them. In the perfect hierarchical society sons should obey their fathers, wives should obey their husbands, the people should obey their emperor and the emperor should obey heaven. The only equal relationship is that between friends. The happiness of society can only be guaranteed if this hierarchy is recognized.

Confucius taught that the contented family is the only foundation for a harmonious world. Parents are expected to teach virtue and duty to their

children, who will grow up respecting them in return. Such respect involves obedience and the unquestioning acceptance of parental authority. Ancestor worship is an expression of the filial obligation and deference that are essential for any cohesive society. The honour given to parents in this life must be continued after death.

Yin and yang

In Confucian thought everything in the universe is made up of two opposite principles: yin (feminine) and yang (masculine). The feminine

Priests conduct Chongmyo *rites at a temple in Seoul, South Korea. In recent years efforts have been made in Korea to reinforce the values of Confucianism in the face of the Westernization of society.*

> *While they [parents] are alive, serve them according to the ritual; when they die bury them according to the ritual; and sacrifice to them according to the ritual.*
> CONFUCIUS, *ANALECTS* 2.5

The opposing principles of yin and yang must be balanced in order to preserve harmony in the universe.

qualities are those which are receptive and yielding, while the masculine qualities are active and unbending. For personal and social contentment these elements must be kept in balance. If an emperor venerates his ancestors in heaven and gains their approval then he will automatically maintain the balance between yin and yang in his kingdom. This in turn will result in good harvests, general prosperity and widespread happiness.

RITUALS AND WORSHIP

Confucianism teaches that all consciousness ends with death. It is a person's duty to revere his or her ancestors and there are special shrines for this, either in the home or in the temple, where offerings are presented. Yet it is this life which is thought to matter most, so Confucianists commemorate events such as births, deaths and, particularly, marriages.

Taoism

The followers of Taoism pursue a spiritual path, or Tao, laid down by ancient Chinese thinkers. The Tao is more than a path, however – it is also the source of everything that exists in the world.

Although its roots can probably be traced back to 2000 BCE, making it China's oldest religion, Taoism itself only emerged towards the end of the first century CE. It takes its name from the Chinese character for 'way' – Tao. The Tao is the primal force in the universe, present in all things yet greater than all things, at the heart of everything in heaven and earth, eternal and unchanging. Since the birth of Taoism, however, the Tao has come to indicate a spiritual path. Taoism draws on elements not only from the ancient Tao tradition but also from Buddhism and Confucianism.

> *The Tao that can be told is not the eternal Tao. The name that can be named is not the eternal name. The nameless is the beginning of heaven and earth... The gate to all mystery.*
>
> LAO-TZU, *TAO TE CHING*

The energy of life

As in Confucianism two natural forces, yin (the feminine) and yang (the masculine), create the energy of life through their interaction with each other. One cannot exist without the other. There cannot be darkness without light, movement without stillness or beauty without ugliness. The dynamic tension between yin and yang creates the Three – heaven, earth and humanity. Heaven and earth are the spiritual and the physical realms while humanity maintains the balance between them. This balance can be disturbed by human wrong-doing and Taoists seek forgiveness for this through their prayers and offerings.

All life is made possible by the *Ch'i*, the life energy, or breath, of the universe. This breath is in everyone and everything from birth to death, so when it expires life itself ceases. Various breathing exercises and yoga are used by Taoists to preserve their *Ch'i* in their quest for immortality. Only by living a balanced life can a constant flow of *Ch'i* be maintained in the body.

Gods and goddesses

Before the Communists took power in China in 1949, almost every Chinese household had its own deities. Although Communism swept most of this 'superstition' away, it returned in the late 1970s when temples were reopened and statues replaced. Although the most popular deities in modern Taoism cover more practical issues such as health, wealth and childbirth the Three Pure Ones of Taoism have also re-emerged:

◆ T'ai-Shang Tao-chun ('august old ruler'), who is often taken to be the legendary Lao-Tzu himself.

◆ T'ai-lao Tao-Chun ('august ruler of the Tao').

◆ Yu-Huang ('jade emperor lord on high').

By giving the gods a setting that imitated the courts of the rulers, heaven was made accessible to ordinary believers.

Annual festivals are essential to Taoism as they reflect the continual renewal of the cosmos. This renewal is celebrated throughout the year, but particularly during winter. Most Taoist festivals also celebrate the birth of a god or heavenly being.

Chinese popular religion draws on Buddhism, Confucianism and Taoism, and all three complement each other. In Taoism almost every aspect of life has its own deity.

Zoroastrianism

The ancient Persian religion of Zoroastrianism teaches that the whole of existence is caught up in the constant struggle between the gods of good and evil.

Zoroastrianism is based on the teachings of Zarathustra, a Persian prophet who is known in the West as Zoroaster. The suggested dates for his birth vary widely between 1200 and 600 BCE, but a likely date is around 1000 BCE. Today Zoroastrianism claims about 200,000 followers; the main communities are in Iran and India.

> *Truly there are two primal spirits, twins renowned to be in conflict. In thought, word and deed they are two: the good and the bad.*
> ZOROASTER, YASNA 30.3

Zoroaster and his teachings

Zoroaster was a practising priest and his teaching is preserved in 17 hymns – the *Gatnas*. Cast in esoteric poetic forms making them difficult to translate, these hymns stem from Zoroaster's conviction that he had seen God, the wise lord Ahura Mazda, in a vision. Zoroastrians worship Ahura Mazda in 'fire temples', where a sacred fire burns continually as a symbol of the deity. Zoroastrians believe that Ahura Mazda created the world and is completely good in his dealings with humankind. His twin, Angra Mainyu, is the god of darkness and destruction, the creator of non-life who produces storms, plagues and monsters as part of his struggle with his brother. This

The wise lord Ahura Mazda, who appeared in visions to Zoroaster, revealed himself as a bountiful sovereign and a friend to everyone.

A 17th-century fire temple in Azerbaijan. Fire has been honoured by Zoroastrians from early times as representing the presence of Ahura Mazda.

dualism lies at the heart of Zoroastrianism.

The eternal fate of each person is determined by the choice they make between Ahura Mazda and Angra Mainyu – a straightforward choice between good and evil. The good enjoy personal happiness in this life and go to heaven, but the evil experience the opposite. Zoroastrians hold strong beliefs in an ultimate resurrection, the final judgment, the torments of hell and the delights of heaven. These beliefs have clear echoes in the eschatology of Judaism, Christianity and Islam. Almost certainly the Wise Men, or Magi, who followed a star from the East to the infant Jesus, were Zoroastrians.

THE PRIEST

The Zoroastrian priesthood is hereditary. It has been maintained over centuries by priestly families, who are traditionally the repositories of religious knowledge. During initiation into the priesthood the initiate dons a sacred cord, reminiscent of Hinduism, and a white shirt to symbolize the constant battle that must be waged against evil and darkness.

Shintoism

The religion of Shintoism reflects the geography and culture of Japan as well as the order and chaos found in the natural world.

Shintoism is indigenous to Japan and means the 'way of the gods'. It was named in the sixth century to distinguish it from Buddhism and Confucianism, which were then recent imports. The worship of *kami* — innumerable gods or spirits — lies at the heart of Shintoism and takes place either at home or at public shrines. Japan boasts thousands of these shrines, catering for the majority of Shintoism's 10 million followers.

Gods, goddesses and spirits

There are thought to be about

The precise origins of Shintoism have been lost with the passing of time. Yet Shintoism has significance for many modern Japanese, who visit shrines to ask the blessing of *kami* on many aspects of life.

RITUALS

At Shinto shrines priests preside over rituals designed to praise a particular *kami* and enlist its support. Worshippers must purify their hands and mouths before worship using water. An offering in the form of a 'horse-picture' is presented, as it is believed horses were messengers of the gods. Amulets bearing the names of the gods are often left as offerings as well. Babies are dedicated at the shrine when they are 13 days old and marriages are also performed there. Funerals, however, are still carried out according to Buddhist rites.

80 million *kami* in Japan but, in the 100,000 or so shrines that are active, some have been given prominence. Amaterasu the sun goddess is the principal *kami* because she rules over heaven. Amaterasu is said to have taught the Japanese how to cultivate rice and to have invented weaving with a loom. She is worshipped as an ancestor as she is believed to have sent her grandson, Ninigi, to found the country's imperial line.

Tenman is worshipped as the god of learning and his

many shrines are popular with students who pray there for success in their exams.

Hachiman was originally the god of farmers but, by the 12th century, he had become the *kami* of war and warriors. There are three major shrines dedicated to Hachiman in Japan – at Usa, Kyoto and Kamakura.

The rice god, Inari, is linked with fertility and prosperity. Stone statues of foxes, his messengers, are usually placed at the entrances to his shrines.

Festivals

There are many festivals in Shintoism and they are held for ancestral, purificatory, exorcism, or agricultural purposes. The central festivals are held at New Year, at rice-planting time in the spring and during the autumn harvest. Spring and autumn are seasons for honouring ancestors and visiting graves. During a festival the *kami* is often carried through the streets in a portable shrine to assure everyone that it is visiting the community to protect it.

The Baha'i Faith

The Baha'i Faith grew out of Islam and is one of the world's newest religions. It presents a worldwide vision of peace and love in a society governed by universal religious principles.

Sayyid' Ali Muhammad (1819–50), a young Shi'ite Muslim, declared himself to be the first in a new line of prophets following on from Muhammad. He called himself the Bab, meaning 'the gateway to God'. In 1848 the Babis, as the followers of Bab were known, declared their independence from Islam and began to fight against the Persian authorities. The Bab was accused of plotting against the Shah of Persia and was executed in 1850.

Baha'ullah

Mirza Husayn Ali was born in Persia in 1817 and was a prominent supporter of the Bab. After the Bab's death Husayn Ali was arrested and put in prison, where he had a mystical experience revealing him to be 'he whom God will make manifest'. When he told his closest friends that he was God's new prophet in 1863, he became known as Baha'ullah, the 'glory of God'. He had already been exiled by the Persian authorities who had felt he posed a threat to them. It was while in exile that Baha'ullah wrote many of the Baha'i texts.

Baha'i teachings

Baha'is believe that God, transcendent and unknowable, has sent many prophets or messengers, to enlighten humanity. Each of these prophets – including Krishna, Buddha, Christ and Muhammad – has founded a world religion. Their messages, however, have been superseded by the written revelations of Baha'ullah and his son and successor, Abdul Baha. Central to Baha'i teaching is the belief that the human race should reach maturity by rejecting any world order that depends on a

Abdul Baha, son of Baha'ullah. Believing that humanity is becoming progressively more mature, father and son wrote down their revelations, which Baha'is believe supersede those of the major figures of other world religions.

The worldwide community of Baha'is is spread across more than 200 countries and thought to total seven million. It is second only to Christianity in the geographical spread of its membership.

> *The Baha'i Faith upholds the unity of God, recognizes the unity of his prophets, and inculcates the principle of the oneness and wholeness of the entire human race.*
>
> SHOGHI EFFENDI

multitude of nations and religions. The world can, and should, be truly one, united behind the spiritual insights of Baha'ullah.

Worship

Prayer is as vital to the Baha'i Faith as it is to Islam and it is carried out daily, usually in the home. Collections of prayers have been passed down from Baha'ullah and Abdul Baha. There are three obligatory prayers, one of which is said every day. Everyone prays facing the direction of Baha'ullah's tomb in Acre, Israel.

There is a strict code of conduct in Baha'ism, based upon the *Kitab I Aqdas*, a book of laws given by Baha'ullah. The fasting month of Ala (March 2–21) is compulsory. Taking drugs and drinking alcohol are strictly forbidden, as are premarital sex and adultery. Marriage is highly valued.

The Baha'i House of Worship at Delhi, India. A house of worship has been built on each of the main continents. They are intended as centres of prayer for people of all faiths, and each has nine entrances, symbolizing nine major faiths.

Rapid Factfinder

Key: Ba = Baha'i Faith; B = Buddhism; C = Christianity; Con = Confucianism; H = Hinduism; I = Islam; J = Judaism; Sh = Shintoism; S = Sikhism; T = Taoism; Z = Zoroastrianism.

A

abbot (C): man traditionally appointed to lead a monastic community.

Abhimdhamma Pitaka (B): commentary on the *Sutta Pitaka*.

Abraham (J): Israelite patriarch believed to be the ancestor of all Jews; accepted as a prophet by Muslims.

absolution (C): the pronouncing of the forgiveness of sins by the priest.

Abu Bakr (I): first Caliph; Muhammad's successor (632–34 CE).

Abu Talib (I): Muhammad's uncle who raised him after he was orphaned.

adhan (I): call to prayer made five times a day by a muezzin from every mosque.

Adi Granth (S): 'first book'; sacred writings compiled by Guru Arjan.

Advent (C): 'coming'; the start of the Christian year; time of penance leading up to Christmas.

Aga Khan (I): leader of the Isma'ilis.

Ahura Mazda (Z): the wise lord, a god of total goodness, opposed to Angra Mainyu.

al-Fatihah (I): the opening surah of the Qur'an.

Aleinu (J): prayer recited at the end of every service in the synagogue.

Allah (I): name of the supreme being worshipped by Muslims.

altar (C): stone table in front of the east wall in a church; platform behind which Communion is conducted.

Amaterasu (Sh): a *kami*; sun goddess and ruler of heaven.

Amidah (J): 'standing'; series of 18 benedictions.

amrit (S): 'holy nectar'; sugared water used in religious services.

Amritsar (S): sacred city in the Punjab in North India; home of the Golden Temple.

Anand (S): composition of Guru Ram Das.

Anand Sahib (S): composition of Guru Ram Amar, included in the *Adi Granth*, used in the *karah parshad* ceremony.

anatta (B): belief that there is no reality underlying appearances so there is no permanent self or soul.

Angel Jibreel (I): God's messenger who appeared to Muhammad; also called the Angel Gabriel.

Anglican Church (C): Church of England and other Episcopal Churches in full communion with the diocese of Canterbury.

Angra Mainyu (Z): god of darkness opposed to Ahura Mazda.

anicca (B): doctrine of impermanence, held to be one of the characteristics of all things.

anti-Semitism (J): attitude of prejudice against the Jewish people.

Anyesti (H): 16th and last samsara relating to funeral rites.

Apocrypha (C): 'hidden'; books written after the Old Testament, included in some Bibles.

apostle (C): 'to send'; name used for the disciples of Jesus after the Day of Pentecost.

Apostles' Creed (C): statement of faith, probably a baptismal confession, dating from the end of the second century.

apostolic order (C): religious community involved in work outside the monastery or convent.

aqiqah (I): ceremony in which the baby's head is shaved and gold or silver equivalent to the weight of the hair is given to the poor.

Ardas (S): formal prayer which is part of a devotional service.

ark (J): cupboard in the synagogue where the scrolls of the Torah are kept.

arti (H): offering of light during *puja*.

Asalha (B): rainy season, during which the Buddha is believed to have taught the Dharma to the gods in heaven.

Ascension Day (C): day for celebrating the ascension of Jesus into heaven.

Ash Wednesday (C): first day of Lent, marked in some Churches by the smearing of ash on the forehead in the form of a cross.

atman (H): the soul or self.

atonement (C): reconciliation between God and human beings through the death and resurrection of Jesus ('at-one-ment').

AUM (H): the sacred syllable.

avatar (H): 'one who descends'; relates to the belief that Vishnu has been incarnated nine times, twice as Rama and Krishna.

Avenue of the Righteous (J): line of trees at Yad Veshem, each representing a Gentile who helped to save a Jew's life during the Holocaust.

ayah (I): a verse in the Qur'an.

B

Baha'i (Ba): follower of the Baha'i Faith.

Baisakhi (S): festival celebrating the birth of the Khalsa in 1699.

baptism (C): rite of initiation into most Christian Churches.

Baptist Church (C): Reformed Church whose distinguishing mark is the baptism of believing adults and not infants.

bar mitzvah (J): 'son of the commandment'; ceremony marking the coming of age of Jewish boy at 13.

bat hayil (J): 'daughter of valour'; Orthodox coming-of-age ceremony for girls around age 12.

bat mitzvah (J): 'daughter of the commandment'; ceremony held in Reform synagogues marking the coming of age of a Jewish girl at the age of 12.

believer's baptism: adult baptism held mainly in Baptist Churches in response to faith in Christ.

Bhagavad Gita (H): 'song of the blessed one'; the most popular Hindu scripture, dating from the fourth or third century BCE.

bhajan (H): hymn sung as part of *puja*.

bhakti (H): 'devotion'; attitude of love towards God which grows into ardent devotion.

bhikku (B): monk or nun.

Bible (C): 'book'; collection of sacred writings believed by many to be divinely inspired.

bimah (J): desk or platform in the synagogue from which the Torah is read.

bishop (C): highest of the three major orders in the Church; given responsibility for a diocese.

Bismillah (I): 'in the name of God, the compassionate, the merciful'; the start of every surah but one in the Qur'an.

Black Stone (I): stone set in the south-east corner of the *Ka'bah*; one of Islam's holiest objects.

bodhi tree (B): tree beneath which Siddharta Gautama became the Buddha, the 'enlightened one'.

Bodhisattva (B): a being who reaches enlightenment but stays behind on earth to help other beings attain the same state.

books of Moses (J): the first five books of the Hebrew scriptures; the Torah.

Brahma (H): creator-god, first member of the *trimurti*, which also includes Vishnu and Shiva.

Brahman (H): the supreme spirit, the absolute.

Brahmin (H): 'twice-born, invested with sacred thread'; the first (white) varna of the highest, priestly caste.

brit milah (J): circumcision ceremony.

Buddha (B): 'enlightened one'; title assumed by Siddharta Gautama after his enlightenment.

Buddhist (B): follower of Buddhism.

C

Caliph (I): 'successor'; title for the leaders of Islam who directly followed Muhammad, of which Abu Bakr was the first.

challah (J): plaited loaf of white, leavened bread baked to celebrate the Sabbath.

charismatic movement (C): movement based on a common belief in the extraordinary experience of the Holy Spirit that has led to renewed freedom of worship in many Churches.

chauri (S): ceremonial whisk, made from the tail hair of a white horse or a yak with a wooden or silver handle, waved over the *Guru Granth Sahib* in the gurdwara.

chevra kadishah (J): group in each synagogue that takes care of people just before and after death.

Ch'i (T): vital energy which pervades and enables all things.

Christian (C): a follower of Jesus Christ.

Christmas (C): festival celebrating the birth of Jesus.

chrismation (C): Orthodox Church service in which immediately follows baptism; equivalent to confirmation.

chuppah (J): canopy beneath which wedding ceremonies take place, symbolizing the home the couple will set up together.

Church of England (C): Church established in England during the Reformation; the established Church in England with the monarch at its head.

Communion (C): sacrament commemorating the death of Jesus, based on the Last Supper.

confessional (C): cubicle in many Catholic churches in which the priest hears confessions.

confirmation (C): service in Episcopalian and other Churches in which a person 'confirms' the vows others made for them when they were baptized as infants.

Confucianist (Con): follower of Confucianism.

Confucius (Con): Latin form of the name Kung Fu-Tzu, the Chinese scholar and philosopher.

contemplative order (C): religious community isolated from the outside world, whose emphasis is on silence, prayer and study.

convent (C): building where nuns live, work, study and pray.

Creed (C): 'I believe'; statement of the tenets of faith.

crucifixion (C): Roman method of execution by which Jesus died.

D

Dalit (H): 'the oppressed'; people of no caste in India.

darshan (H): being in the presence of God.

Day of Atonement (C): Yom Kippur; the most solemn day in the Jewish year.

Day of Judgment (I): when Allah will judge each Muslim according to his or her deeds.

Day of Pentecost (C): festival celebrating when God gave the Ten Commandments to Moses on Mount Sinai; day when the Holy Spirit was poured out on the early Church.

deacon (C): lowest of the three orders of ministry in the Church, below bishop and priest.

Dharma (B): the Buddha's teaching, one of the Three Refuges.

Diaspora (J): dispersion of Jews throughout the world.

Divali (H, S): festival of lights; New Year festival.

Divine Liturgy (C): the Orthodox Church's term for the service which includes the sacrament of Communion.

diwan (S): 'royal court'; main room of the gurdwara; act of worship.

Dome of the Rock (I): mosque in Jerusalem, built on the site where the Jewish Temple stood.

du'a (I): private prayer.

dukkha (B): 'suffering'; first of the Four Noble Truths.

E

Easter (C): festival commemorating Jesus' death and resurrection.

Eastern Orthodox Church (C): Church which is dominant in Eastern Europe.

Eightfold Path (B): Middle Way; eight steps towards nirvana, laid down by the Buddha, which lie between the extremes of asceticism and sensuality.

Epiphany (C): 'manifestation'; festival on 6 January celebrating Jesus' appearance in the world.

Episcopalian Church: name given to the Anglican Church in the USA, Canada and Scotland.

Eucharist (C): 'thanksgiving'; alternative name for Communion, often used by Anglicans.

exodus (J): the time when Moses led the Israelites from slavery in Egypt to freedom in the Promised Land of Canaan.

extreme unction (C): the anointing of the sick and dying, one of the seven sacraments of the Roman Catholic Church, now called 'anointing of the sick'.

F

Festival of the Sacred Tooth (B): festival linked with a relic of the Buddha, in Kandy, Sri Lanka.

fire altar (H): altar on which fire is offered to a god.

fire temple (Z): where a sacred fire continually burns.

Five Faithful Ones (S): as *panj piares*.

Five Ks (S): the symbols worn by Sikhs who have been initiated into the Khalsa.

Five Pillars of Islam (I): the five fundamental beliefs of Islam.

Five Precepts (B): moral guidelines.

font (C): 'spring of water'; stone container used to hold water for infant baptism.

forest monks (B): strict monastic order believed to be closest of all to enlightenment.

Former Prophets (J): historical books of the *TeNaKh*, found in the Prophets.

Four Noble Truths (B): the knowledge of suffering, the source of suffering, the removal of suffering and the way to remove suffering.

Four Rightly Guided Caliphs (I): name given by Sunni Muslims to the first four Muslim leaders after Muhammad; the first three are not recognized by Shi'ite Muslims.

Friday Prayers (I): the main service of the week, held in the mosque, which all males Muslims must attend.

G

Ganesha (H): elephant-headed god, son of Shiva and Parvati, god of wisdom and good fortune.

garbhagrha (H): inner room of the temple, the holiest part where the image of the god is installed.

Gatnas (Z): 17 hymns preserving the teachings of Zoroaster.

Siddharta Gautama (B): prince who became the Buddha through enlightenment.

Gemara (J): 'completion'; commentry on the Mishnah included in the Talmud.

Gentile (J): a person who is not Jewish.

ghat (H): steps leading down to a river; landing place.

Golden Temple (S): built by Guru Arjan beside the Pool of Immortality in Amritsar.

Good Friday (C): day in Holy Week when Christians remember the death of Jesus on the cross.

gospel (C): 'good news' of Jesus.

Gospels (C): four books in the New Testament which describe the life and teaching of Jesus.

granthi (S): man or woman who looks after the *Guru Granth Sahib* in a gurdwara; duties include reading the scriptures and recitation of prayers.

gurdwara (S): 'the door of the Guru'; temple or building used for corporate acts of worship.

gurmukh (S): one whose life is inspired by the teachings of the Gurus.

Gurmukhi (S): 'from the Guru's mouth'; sacred script devised by Guru Angad; language of the *Guru Granth Sahib* that placed these scriptures within everyone's reach.

gurpurb (S): festival commemorating the birth or death of a Guru.

Guru (H): holy man, woman or teacher.

Guru Amar Das (S): third Guru, who instituted distinctive ceremonies and festivals as well as places of pilgrimage.

Guru Angad (S): second Guru, chosen to be Guru Nanak's successor in preference to Guru Nanak's son.

Guru Arjan (S): fifth Guru, who built the Golden Temple in Amritsar (the *Harimandir*); the only Guru to be martyred.

Guru Gobind Singh (S): tenth and final Guru, responsible for founding the Khalsa.

Guru Granth Sahib (S): holy book containing the *Adi Granth* and other writings; declared the 11th Guru by Guru Gobind Singh.

Guru Har Gobind (S): sixth Guru.

Guru Har Krishan (S): eighth Guru.

Guru Har Rai (S): seventh Guru.

Guru Nanak (S): first Guru and founder of the Sikh community; his teachings are found in the *Guru Granth Sahib*.

Guru Ram Das (S): fourth Guru, remembered for founding the holy city of Amritsar.

Guru Tegh Bahadur (S): ninth Guru.

Gyatri Mantra (H): most sacred verse in the *Rig Veda*, repeated by Hindus on rising, at noon and before sleeping.

H

Hachiman (Sh): *kami* of war.

Hagadah (J): 'telling'; book used during the Seder meal at Passover to recount the story of the exodus from Egypt.

Hail Mary (C): Roman Catholic prayer to the Virgin Mary, also called the 'Ave Maria'.

Hajar (I): wife of the prophet Ibrahim, mother of Isma'il, known in Jewish and Christian traditions as Hagar.

Hajj (I): the pilgrimage to Makkah; one of the Five Pillars of Islam.

hajjah (I): a woman who has completed the Hajj.

hajji (I): a man who has completed the Hajj.

halal (I): any food that a Muslim is permitted to eat.

Hanukkah (J): eight-day festival celebrating the victory of Judas Maccabeus over Antiochus IV, also called the festival of lights.

Hanuman (H): major character in the *Ramayana*, monkey-king who helped rescue Sita from Ravana's kingdom of Lanka.

haram (I): things that a Muslim is not permitted to do.

Harijans (H): 'untouchables'; the fifth and lowest group in Indian society.

Harimandir (S): 'temple of God'; ascribed to several Sikh shrines but particularly the Golden Temple.

Hasidism (J): 17th-century movement which stressed the value of piety over learning.

havan (H): fire offering.

Havdalah (J): 'separation'; ceremony ending the Sabbath day.

High Priest (J): Jewish leader during the time of the Roman occupation of Palestine.

Hijrah (I): 'emigration'; Muhammad's journey from Makkah to Madinah in 622 CE; beginning of the Islamic calendar.

Hindu (H): follower of Hinduism.

Hola Mohalla (S): 'attack or be attacked'; festival celebrating miltary prowess; traditionally a day of military training through the fighting of mock battles.

Holi (H): five-day festival celebrated in the spring commemorating the avatar of Krishna.

Holocaust (J): 'burnt offering'; the slaughter of six million Jews by the Nazis in the Second World War.

Holy of Holies (J): innermost part of Solomon's Temple where the original ark of the covenant was kept.

holy orders (C): people who are ordained: bishop, priests and deacons.

Holy Spirit (C): the third member of the Trinity; God active in the world today.

Holy Week (C): last week of Lent, beginning with Palm Sunday and leading up to Easter Sunday.

host (C): 'sacrifice'; bread used in the Roman Catholic Mass.

hukam (S): divine order, in which nothing in the world is exempt from God's control.

I

Iblis (I): Satan, the angel who disobeyed Allah by not bowing to Adam and became the tempter of humankind.

icon (C): special painting of the Jesus, the Virgin Mary or a saint used as an aid to prayer by Orthodox believers.

Id-ul-Adha (I): festival at which animals are sacrificed during the Hajj.

ihram (I): white cloths worn by male pilgrims during the Hajj.

imam (I): man who leads public worship in a mosque; leaders of Shi'ite Muslims.

incarnation (C): belief that God was born as a human in the form of Jesus.

infant baptism (C): the practice of many Churches of baptizing babies.

Isma'ilis (I): group associated with Shi'ite Muslims although they have many distinctive teachings of their own.

J

Japji (S): hymn by Guru Gobind Singh; introductory invocation to the *Dasam Granth*.

Japji Sahib (S): long poem composed by Guru Nanak; recited daily by devout Sikhs.

Jerusalem (J, I, C): sacred city in Israel.

Jesus Prayer (C): 'Lord Jesus Christ, Son of God, have mercy on me, a sinner'; used as a mantra by Orthodox Christians.

Jew (J): one of Hebrew descent; follower of Judaism.

jihad (I): holy war which can be fought by Muslims if certain strict conditions are met.

jnana (H): path of knowledge; a way of approaching Brahman.

John the Baptist (C): man sent by God to prepare the way for the coming of Jesus.

K

Ka'bah (I): 'the house of God'; cube-shaped shrine in Makkah; focus of the Hajj.

kachera (S): shorts worn by members of the Khalsa; one of the five Ks.

Kaddish (J): prayer of sanctification often used as part of Jewish mourning rites.

kami (Sh): gods, goddesses, spirits or superior beings.

kangha (S): wooden comb worn by members of the Khalsa; one of the five Ks.

kara (S): steel bracelet worn by members of the Khalsa; one of the five Ks.

karah parshad (S): sanctified food which is distributed at ceremonies.

karma (H, B): 'doing'; present deeds which determine one's destiny in a future life; an unbreakable law.

kashrut (J): dietary laws.

Kathina (B): festival of giving to monks.

kesh (S): the long, uncut hair of members of the Khalsa, tied in a knot; one of the five Ks.

ketubah (J): marriage document received by the bride which outlines the groom's duties in married life.

Khalsa (S): brotherhood founded by Guru Gobind Singh in 1699; the Sikh community.

khanda (S): two-edged sword representing power and divinity; used in the *amrit* ceremony.

kirpan (S): short knife carried by members of the Khalsa; a symbol of active resistance to evil; one of the five Ks.

kirtan (S): devotional singing of hymns from the *Guru Granth Sahib*.

koan (B): 'riddle'; term used in Zen Buddhism for a word or phrase which cannot be understood or solved by the intellect.

kosher (J): the categories of food which Jews are permitted to eat.

Krishna (H): one of the most popular Hindu gods, an avatar of Vishnu.

Kshatriya (H): second highest caste in India; the red varna comprising warriors and rulers.

Kumbh Mela (H): impressive festival held every 12 years, involving vast numbers of people.

L

langar (S): kitchen attached to a gurdwara where the congregation enjoys a communal meal after *diwan*.

last rites (C): traditional rites performed by the Catholic priest over a person before they die.

Last Supper (C): the last meal Jesus ate with his disciples before his crucifixion; pattern for the sacrament of Communion.

Latter Prophets (J): prophetic books of the *TeNaKh*, found in the Prophets.

The Laws of Manu (H): law code attributed to the legendary figure of Manu, the first man.

Lehna (S): devoted follower chosen by Guru Nanak to succeed him as the Sikh leader who became Guru Angad.

Lent (C): forty days of repentance before Easter.

Liberation Theology (C): a theology developed in South America by Roman Catholic and Protestant theologians, emphasizing that the Christian gospel is for the poor.

Liturgy of the Eucharist (C): part of the Catholic Mass in which the priest consecrates the bread and wine before Communion.

Liturgy of the Word (C): part of the Catholic Mass which includes three Bible readings, a sermon and the Nicene Creed.

Lord's Prayer (C): the prayer that Jesus taught his disciples; the only prayer used in Churches of all denominations and traditions.

Lord's Supper (C): popular name among Reformed Churches for the sacrament of Communion.

lotus position (B): basic position in yoga meditation.

Lutheran Church (C): Protestant denomination strong in Germany, Scandinavia and the USA that follows the teachings of Martin Luther in theology and Church organization.

M

Madinah (I): the second sacred city of Islam, 300 miles from Makkah.

madrassah (I): school held in the mosque for teaching Muslim children about the Qur'an and how to read it in Arabic.

Mahabharata (H): epic poem, written in the second or third century BCE, containing almost 100,000 verses.

Mahayana Buddhism (B): 'the great vehicle'; branch of Buddhism which takes as its ideal the Bodhisattva, or seeking enlightenment.

Makkah (I): birthplace of Muhammad, the most sacred site in Islam; home of the *Ka'bah*.

mala: (B): prayer beads.

mandala (H): complex geometric pattern used in worship.

mandapa (H): main area of the temple.

mandir (H): temple.

mantra (H): words or short phrases which are repeated incessantly during meditation to free the mind from illusion, or *maya*.

Marwah (I): hill near Makkah, twinned with Safa; pilgrims run between the hills during the Hajj.

Mass (C): Roman Catholic term for the service which includes the sacrament of Communion.

matzah loaves (J): unleavened bread.

Maundy Thursday (C): day before Good Friday, on which Jesus ate the Last Supper, washed his disciples' feet and commanded them to love one another.

megillah (J): scroll of the book of Esther read during the festival of Purim.

mela (S): 'fairs'; festivals such as Baisakhi, Divali and *Hola Mohalla*.

menorah (J): seven-branched candlestick used in the Jerusalem Temple; found in every Jewish home and synagogue.

Messiah (C, J): deliverer expected by Jews for centuries; his coming was prophesied in the Old Testament; Christians believe Jesus Christ was the Messiah.

Methodist Church (C): Church founded on the teachings of John Wesley in the 18th century.

mezuzah (J): small parchment scroll inscribed with two passages from the Torah, enclosed in a box and attached to the doorposts of most rooms in the Jewish home.

Middle Way (B): the path marked out by the Buddha avoiding the extremes of asceticism and indulgence.

mihrab (I): arched alcove or niche in the wall of a mosque indicating the direction of Makkah.

minaret (I): the tower of the mosque from which the muezzin calls the faithful to prayer five times a day.

minbar (I): set of three steps in the mosque from which the imam preaches at Friday Prayers.

minister (C): ordained Protestant Church leader.

Minor Prophets (J): last section of the Prophets, the second book of the *TeNaKh*.

minyan (J): quorum of 10 males which, according to Orthodox Judaism, needs to be present before prayers can be offered.

misbeha (I): prayer beads to assist Muslims in recalling the 99 beautiful names of Allah.

Mishnah (J): oral law; supplementary laws given by God on Mount Sinai and passed down for centuries by word of mouth; part of the Talmud.

mitzvah, mitzvot (J): 'commandment'; any religious duty.

Modern Orthodox (J): Jews who believe in a synthesis between the Torah and Western ideas.

mohel (J): trained Jewish circumciser.

moksha (H): release or salvation, liberation from the cycle of rebirth, through knowledge, works or devotion.

monks (B, C): male members of a Buddhist community, or *Sangha*, whose earnest focus is on reaching enlightenment; members of a Christian all-male religious order who live together in a monastery.

Mool Mantar (S): 'basic teaching'; one of the first compositions of Guru Nanak, which expresses the tenets of the faith and appears at the start of the *Guru Granth Sahib*.

Moses (J): leader of the exodus from Egypt who received the Ten Commandments from God on Mount Sinai.

mosque (I): building used for public prayers, containing a place for washing, an open prayer area and a *mihrab*.

mother superior (C): leader of a female religious order.

muezzin (I): man who calls Muslims to prayer five times a day by chanting the *adhan* from the minaret.

Muhammad (I): Islam's founder; the last and greatest prophet of Allah.

murti (H): the embodied form of a god, the visible image.

Muslim (I): 'one who submits to Allah'; follower of Islam.

N

ner tamid (J): 'eternal lamp'; light which burns perpetually in front of the ark in the synagogue.

New Testament (C): canonical books of the Church, including the Gospels and the epistles.

Nicene Creed (C): statement of belief drawn up by the Council of Nicea in 325 CE.

nirvana (B): 'to blow out'; place where sin or self is 'blown out' or becomes extinct.

Nishan Sahib (S): flag which flies outside the gurdwara.

nuptial Mass (C): Mass celebrated by the groom and bride alone at the end of a Roman Catholic wedding ceremony.

O

Old Testament (C): books of the Jewish scriptures incorporated into the Christian Bible.

oral tradition (C): way in which information was kept alive by word of mouth before it was written down.

Orthodox Church (C): originally the Church of the eastern part of the Roman empire, separated from the Roman Catholic Church in 1054, now divided into many branches.

Orthodox Jew (J): a Jew who holds to the traditions of the Jewish faith handed down from the distant past.

P

Pali Canon (B): canonical scriptures of Theravada Buddhism; comprises the *Vinaya Pitaka, Sutta Pitaka* and *Abhidamma Pitaka.*

Palm Sunday (C): day at the beginning of Holy Week celebrating the triumphal entry of Jesus in Jerusalem on a donkey.

panj piares (S): the original five members of the Khalsa.

parable (C): a form of teaching used by Jesus, with elements taken from everyday life used to illustrate religious morals.

Passover (J): annual festival at which Jews remember the deliverance of the Israelites from Egyptian slavery.

patit (S): lapsed member.

Paul (C): persecutor of the early Church, converted to Christ on the Damascus Road, tireless missionary, writer of many New Testament epistles.

penance (C): one of seven sacraments recognized by the Roman Catholic Church; the payment of a penalty to guarantee forgiveness of sins.

Pentecost (J, C): Jewish festival of Shavuot, the Feast of Weeks, which was being celebrated when the Holy Spirit was poured out on the Christian Church.

Pentecostal Church (C): Widespread movement among Protestants whose emphasis is on experience of the Holy Spirit.

Pesach (J): as Passover.

Peter (C): disciple of Jesus, leader of the early Church, believed by Roman Catholics to have been the first Pope (the Bishop of Rome).

phylactery (J): as *tefillin.*

Pontius Pilate (C): Roman governor (26–36 CE) who ordered the crucifixion of Jesus.

Pool of Immortality (S): lake in Amritsar, at the centre of which sits the Golden Temple.

Pope (C): Bishop of Rome; chief bishop and leader of the Roman Catholic Church.

prashad (H): sacred food offered to a god in the temple.

prayer mat (I): used during prayer in the mosque.

prayer wheel (B): wheel used in Tibetan monasteries and temples, inscribed with prayers or sacred phrases.

priest (C): 'elder'; man or woman ordained by a bishop in the Orthodox, Roman Catholic and Anglican Church, authorized to dispense the sacraments.

Progressive Judaism (J): a form of Judaism whose followers believe that tradition must be brought into line with modern ideas.

Promised Land (J): land of Canaan promised to the Jewish ancestors after leaving slavery in Egypt.

Prophets (J): second division of the *TeNaKh,* positioned after the Torah and before the Writings; divided into the Former Prophets and the Latter Prophets. Also called *Nevi'im*.

Protestant Church (C): Church which does not owe allegiance to either the Roman Catholic Church or the Orthodox Church.

puja (H): worship or reverence of the gods; offering of gifts to the *murti*.

pulpit (C): elevated stand at the front of the church from which sermons are delivered.

purgatory (C): Roman Catholic concept of a place after death for people not yet ready to enter heaven.

Purim (J): festival celebrating the success of Esther in saving many Jews from massacre by their enemy Haman.

Q

qiblah (I): direction marked by the *mihrab* towards which Muslims must pray, facing the *Ka'bah* in Makkah.

Quakers (C): movement formed by George Fox in the 17th century emphasizing nonviolence and silence in worship; also called the 'Society of Friends'.

Qu'ran (I): sacred book of Islam recording revelations given to Muhammad by the Angel Jibreel.

R

rabbi (J): 'my master'; title given to an authorized teacher in the synagogue or Jewish community.

rak'ah (I): part of the *salah*; a sequence of movements and quotations from the Qur'an.

Ramadan (I): ninth month of the Muslim calendar, during which all Muslims must fast from dawn until sunset.

Ramayana (H): epic poem in Sanskrit attributed to the sage Valmiki in the fifth century BCE.

Rasul (I): 'messenger of Allah'; title given to Muhammed in a revelation from God.

rebbe (J): spiritual leader of Hasidic Jews.

Reformation (C): movement started in 1517 by Martin Luther in Germany that led to the formation of many Protestant Churches.

Reformed Churches (C): term loosely applied to all Protestant Churches.

reincarnation (H, B): belief that, after death, the soul lives again on earth in another body.

religious orders (C): monks or nuns living together according to a common discipline or rule.

resurrection (C): the rising from death of Jesus, on the third day after his crucifixion, and of all believers on the Day of Judgment.

Rig Veda (H): 'verse knowledge'; the most sacred and ancient Hindu scriptures.

River Indus (H): site of the origins of Hinduism among the Indus people, whose Sanskrit name, *Siddhu*, gave rise to the term 'Hindu'.

Roman Catholic Church (C): worldwide community of believers with allegiance to the Pope; the largest Christian denomination.

Rosh Hashanah (J): New Year, marked by the blowing of the shofar, which inaugurates 10 days of penitence ending with the Day of Atonement.

S

Sabbath day (J): holy day of rest, when all work ceases, running from Friday evening to Saturday evening; sometimes called Shabbat.

Sacrament of Reconciliation (C): Roman Catholic sacrament offering forgiveness of sins.

sadaqah (I): voluntary donations and gifts; additional to *zakah*.

sadhsangat (S): congregation.

sadhu (H): Sanskrit for 'holy man'; sage or ascetic.

Safa (I): low mound at Makkah, twinned with Marwah; pilgrims run backwards and forwards between Marwah and Safa seven times on the Hajj.

salah (I): ritual or liturgical prayer observed five times a day; second of the Five Pillars of Islam.

Salvation Army (C): Protestant organization, formed by William and Catherine Booth in 1878, emphasizing social work as part of the Christian message.

samadhi (H): contemplation.

samatha (B): a type of meditation.

samsara (H): the world, the place where the cycle of birth, life and death takes place.

samskara (H): life-cycle ceremonies such as the sacred-thread ceremony.

Sangha (B): community of monks instituted by Buddha; one of the Three Refuges.

Sanhedrin (C): highest Jewish Court, with 71 members, that met in Jerusalem at the time of Jesus.

sawm (I): period of fasting during Ramadan; the third Pillar of Islam.

Satan (C): 'accuser'; leader of evil spirits opposed to God; tempter of Jesus.

Second Coming (C): belief that Jesus will return to the earth at some future time.

Second Vatican Council (C): meeting of the Pope with Catholic bishops in Rome between 1962 and 1965 that introduced many changes in Church worship.

Seder (J): 'order'; meal eaten at the start of Passover.

Sefer Torah (J): scroll of the Torah kept in the ark.

Shabbat (J): as Sabbath.

Shahadah (I): first Pillar of Islam; statement of belief in Allah and Muhammad, his prophet.

Shavuot (J): as Pentecost.

shechita (J): rules for preparing food to make it kosher.

Shema (J): prayer and statement of belief in one God.

Shi'ite Muslims (I): group rejecting the claims of the three Caliphs after Muhammad to be the true leaders of the faith.

Shiva (H): the destroyer; god making up the *trimurti* of gods with Brahma and Vishnu.

Shoah (J): 'desolation'; suffering and murder of European Jews by the Nazis during the Holocaust.

shofar (J): ram's-horn trumpet used to usher in New Year (Rosh Hashanah) and the Day of Atonement (Yom Kippur).

Shruti (H): 'that which is heard'; sacred writings including the *Vedas*.

Siddur (J): daily prayer book; used in worship.

Sikh (S): 'disciple'; follower of Sikhism.

Sikh Gurdwara Act (S): act passed in 1925 in which a Sikh is defined.

Simchat Torah (J): 'rejoicing in the law'; festival marking the end of one cycle of readings from the Torah in the synagogue and the beginning of the next.

Smriti (H): 'that which is remembered'; holy books.

Son of God (C): one of the titles given to Jesus in the Gospels.

Son of man (C): one of the titles given to Jesus in the Gospels.

State of Israel (J): established in 1948.

Sudra (H): the fourth (black) varna; the workers, the lowest caste in Indian society.

Sukkot (J): the Feast of Tabernacles; one of the three Jewish 'pilgrimage' festivals.

Sunday (C): holy day set aside for worship.

Sunnah (I): 'path'; tradition, theory and practice of Sunni Muslims as laid down by Muhammad from which they derive their name.

Sunni Muslims (I): Muslims reliant on the Qur'an, the *Sunnah* and the community for the integrity of their faith.

surah (I): a chapter in the Qur'an.

Sutta Pitaka (B): second of three collections of the Buddha's teachings in the *Pali Canon*.

synagogue (J): place of prayer and study.

synoptic Gospels (C): 'seeing together'; the three Gospels of Matthew, Mark and Luke, which have a similar approach to the life of Jesus and much material in common.

T

Taittiriya Upanishad (H): one of the *Upanishads*, explaining the teachings of the *Vedas*.

takht (S): throne on which the *Guru Granth Sahib* sits in a gurdwara.

tallit (J): prayer shawl of white material with fringes, worn by males during morning synagogue services and at all services on the Day of Atonement.

Talmud (J): major source of the Jewish law, made up of the Mishnah and the Gemara.

Tao (T): spiritual path and source of all that exists in the world.

Taoist (T): follower of Taoism.

Tathagata (H): 'gone thus'; a title of the Buddha.

tawaf (I): custom of walking seven times around the *Ka'bah* during the Hajj.

tawhid (I): belief in the oneness of Allah.

tefillin (J): two boxes of leather containing passages from the Torah, fastened by straps to the forehead and left arm; also called phylacteries.

Temple (J): building erected by Solomon around 950 BCE for the worship of God destroyed by the Babylonians in 586 BCE. The second Temple was destroyed by the Romans in 70 CE.

Ten Commandments (C, J): laws given to Moses by God on Mount Sinai, also known as the Ten Sayings.

Ten Gurus (S): teachers and spiritual leaders, starting with Guru Nanak, the founder of the faith, and ending with Guru Gobind Singh, the last human Guru.

TeNaKh (J): colloquial term for the Jewish scriptures.

Tenman (Sh): god of learning.

Theravada Buddhism (B): one of the main groups in Buddhism; claims to follow teachings of the Elders with a conservative approach; the way of the monks.

Three Pure Ones (T): T'ai-Shang Lao-chun, T'ai-lao Tao-Chun and Yu-Huang.

Three Refuges (B): the Buddha, the Dharma and the *Sangha*.

Tibetan Book of the Dead (B): one of several recently discovered books relating to the afterlife.

Tipitaka (B): 'three baskets'; the three sections of the *Pali Canon*, accepted by Theravada Buddhists.

Torah (J): 'law' or 'teaching'; applies to the law of Moses – Genesis, Exodus, Leviticus,

Deuteronomy and Numbers in Jewish scriptures.

transubstantiation (C): Roman Catholic belief that the bread and wine turn into the actual body and blood of Jesus during the Mass.

trimurti (H): 'the three deities'; Brahma, Vishnu and Shiva.

Trinity (C): belief that there is one God in three persons – God the Father, God the Son and God the Holy Spirit.

U

Ultra-Orthodox Jew (J): one who interprets Jewish customs and traditions very strictly.

Ummah (I): worldwide Muslim community.

upanayana (H): sacred-thread ceremony, the most important of the samskaras.

Upanishads (H): 'sit down near a teacher'; holy book derived from sessions where disciples sat listening at the feet of the Gurus.

Uposatha days (H): 'entering to stay'; linked with the phases of the moon and other special days in the lunar calendar.

V

Vaishya (H): third (yellow) varna, of farmers and merchants.

Varanasi (H): the most sacred Hindu pilgrimage site, formerly known as Benares.

varna (H) 'colour'; each of the four castes into which Indian society is traditionally divided is assigned a colour or varna: white, red, yellow or black.

Vedas (H): 'knowledge'; four books – the *Rig Veda*, the *Sama Veda*, the *Yajur Veda* and the *Atharva Veda* – written between 1500 and 800 BCE.

viaticum (C): last Communion taken by a Roman Catholic before death.

vihara (B): a permanent Buddhist monastery.

Vimalakirti Sutra (B): part of the Mahayana scriptures, authoritative as the word of Buddha.

Vinaya Pitaka (B): one of three sections of the *Pali Canon*.

Vipassana (I): form of meditation designed to yield insight into truth.

Virgin Mary (C): Mother of Jesus, given special devotion by Roman Catholics and Orthodox believers.

Vishnu (H): the preserver, associated with Brahma and Shiva in the *trimurti*.

W

Wesak (B): full-moon festival commemorating the birth, enlightenment and death of the Buddha.

Western Wall (J): place of pilgrimage for Jews in Jerusalem; only part of the Temple still remaining.

Whitsun (C): festival celebrating the giving of the Holy Spirit to the apostles at Pentecost.

Writings (J): third part of the *TeNaKh*, after the Torah and the Prophets; also called *Ketuvim*.

wudu (I): washing ritual which takes place before *salah*.

Y

yad (J): hand-held pointer used when reading the *Sefer Torah*.

yakudoshi (Sh): 'unlucky year'; time when believers undergo purification and seek protection in the form of amulets.

yarmulke (J): skullcap.

Yin and Yang (Con): Chinese philosophy that everything in the universe depends on two opposing principles, the male principle, which is light and positive, and the female principle, which is dark and negative.

yoga (B, H): 'yoke'; method of self-control and discipline leading to salvation.

Yom Kippur (J): as Day of Atonement, the most solemn day in the Jewish year.

Z

zakah (I): 'almsgiving'; the third of Five Pillars of Islam; tax levied to help the poor and needy.

Zoroaster (Z): Greek form of Zarathustra, the Iranian prophet and reformer of the 10th century BCE, who founded Zoroastrianism.

Zoroastrian (Z): follower of Zoroastrianism.

Picture Acknowledgments

The Bodleian Library, University of Oxford: p. 101 (ms. douce 144, fol. 111v).

Susanna Burton: pp. 18, 75, 84–85, 98, 128, 134–35, 155 (top).

Cephas Picture Library: p. 112 (bottom, Kensington Temple: Jim Loring/Cephas).

Christie's Images Ltd: p. 89 (*Christ en Croix* [aquatint printed in colours, 1936] by Georges Roualt [1871–1958], copyright © ADAGP, Paris and DACS, London, 2001).

Circa Photo Library: pp. 10, 56 (Barrie Searle), 73 (William Holtby), 136 (John Smith), 176–77 (Martin Palmer).

Hutchison Picture Library: pp. 13 (Hindu priest, Calcutta, copyright © Nick Haslam), 37 (Hindu temple, Madras, copyright © Maurice Harvey), 51 (cutting challah, copyright © Liba Taylor), 70–71 (monks on alms rounds, Shwe Kyetyet, Myanmar, copyright © R. Ian Lloyd), 76, 86–87 (hillside cross, Seychelles, copyright © Goycolea), 110 (Christian funeral, Western Samoa, copyright © Michael MacIntyre), 115 (Russian Orthodox Easter celebration, Tobolsk, copyright © Andrey Zvoznikov), 116, 119 (San Francisco worshippers, Glide Memorial United Methodist Church, copyright © Melanie Friend), 142–43 (Bedouin meal, Bahrain, copyright © Bernard Gerard), 162–63 (new-temple ceremony, Kenya), 170 (*Chongmyo* rites, Seoul), 175 (fire-worshippers' temple, Surakhany, copyright © Trevor Page).

Jon Arnold Images: pp. 38–39.

Alex Keene (The Walking Camera): pp. 14, 16, 21, 23, 24, 26, 28–29, 31, 33, 34–35, 42–43, 45, 48, 50, 53, 55, 59, 61, 62, 65, 69, 80–81, 93, 94, 104, 106, 107, 108, 131, 133 (top), 134 (top), 140, 148, 153, 155 (bottom), 156–57, 158, 158–59, 160, 161, 164–65.

Lion Publishing: pp. 2 (both), 2–3, 3 (David Townsend), 4–5 (David Townsend), 5, 6, 7 (both), 22, 54 (David Townsend), 82, 99 (Ffotograff/Patricia Aithie), 102 (Phil Manning), 105, 112 (top), 118, 130 (David Townsend), 168–69, 171, 173, 174 (Joshua Smith), 179.

The MacQuitty International Photographic Collection: pp. 146–47 (Golden Temple, Amritsar).

The National Gallery, London: p. 90 (*Jesus Opens the Eyes of a Man Born Blind* [tempera on wood] by Duccio di Buoninsegna [c. 1255–c. 1318]).

Peter Sanders Photography Ltd: pp. 120–21, 122–23, 125, 138–39, 144–45, 166–67.

John Rogers: p. 117 (photograph © John Rogers).

Topham Picturepoint: pp. 3 (bottom, Golden Temple, Amritsar), 8–9 (Benares waterfront), 17 (Ganesha idol), 25 (*puja*), 41 (menorah from a *Haggadah*), 46 (synagogue, Jerusalem), 66–67, 79 (temple of the Sera Monastery), 97 (St Peter's Cathedral, Vatican, Rome), 109 (baptism at Fuente de Vida Pentecostal Church, Havana, January 1998, copyright © Michael A. Schwarz/The Image Works), 127 (priest at theological college, Shiraz), 133 (bottom, mosque of Sokulli Mehmet Paça, Istanbul), 141 (Muslim burial ceremony, Shiraz), 151 (Sikh boys march in New Delhi on the anniversary of the death of Guru Tegh Bahadur), 165 (Golden Temple, Amritsar), 178 (Abdul Baha).

Alan Walden: p. 103.

Derek West: front and back endpapers.